Alpha Mathematics 3
New Edition

Compiled by
T. R. Goddard,
J. W. Adams and R. P. Beaumont

 Schofield & Sims Ltd Huddersfield

0 7217 2252 0

First printed 1979

Reprinted 1979

Reprinted 1980

Reprinted 1981

The books in the two series forming this programme comprise:

Ready for Alpha and Beta 0 7217 2266 0

Beta Mathematics 1	Alpha Mathematics 1
0 7217 2258 X	0 7217 2250 4
Beta Mathematics 2	Alpha Mathematics 2
0 7217 2259 8	0 7217 2251 2
Beta Mathematics 3	Alpha Mathematics 3
0 7217 2260 1	0 7217 2252 0
Beta Mathematics 4	Alpha Mathematics 4
0 7217 2261 X	0 7217 2253 9
Beta Mathematics 5	
0 7217 2268 7	
Beta Mathematics 6	
0 7217 2269 5	

Designed by Peter Sinclair (Design and Print) Ltd, Wetherby

Printed in England by Chorley & Pickersgill Ltd, Leeds

Contents　Alpha Mathematics 3

Decimal number system

A Read the numbers in the table and write them in words.

Th	H	T	U	t	h
1			5	0 . 7	
2			9 . 0	4	
3	3	0	7	0	
4			0 . 8	3	

Draw a similar table and write in these numbers, putting the decimal point in the correct place.

5 ninety point nought eight

6 seven thousand and nineteen

7 four hundred and two point six

8 eleven point five nine

Write and complete the following.

9

426.5
= ☐ hundreds ☐ tens ☐ units ☐ tenths
= ☐ tens ☐ units ☐ tenths
= ☐ units ☐ tenths
= ☐ tenths

10

39.78
= 3 tens 9 units 7 tenths 8 hundredths
= 9 units 7 tenths 8 hundredths
= 9 tenths 8 hundredths
= 27 hundredths

B Write answers only to the following.

1 3000+500+80+6

2 8000+700

3 4000+5

4 40+8+5 tenths+7 hundredths

5 5000+70+9 tenths

6 90+7+11 hundredths

7 20+83 hundredths

8 300+7 hundredths

9 2000+45 tenths

10 3+118 hundredths

Write the value of each figure underlined.

11 30_8_.2   12 _8_604   13 70._8_5

14 9_0_27   15 7_2_03   16 19._0_2

Write the numbers below. Put in decimal points so that the value of each 8 is 80.

17 8463   18 95824   19 800

Write the numbers below. Put in decimal points so that the value of the 7 is 7 tenths.

20 37   21 117   22 579   23 70

Write the numbers below. Put in decimal points so that the value of each 5 is 5 hundredths.

24 115   25 1325   26 45   27 2005

C

	Thousands				
	H	T	U	H	T	U
	Hundred thousands	Ten thousands	Thousands	Hundreds	Tens	Units
1		4	6	1	3	9
2	5	7	3	8	5	4
3		2	0	3	1	7
4	3	0	9	0	4	6
5	7	0	0	6	3	0

Read the numbers in the table to your partner who will check them from the answer book.

Write each of these numbers in figures.

6 four thousand seven hundred and fifty-three

7 thirty thousand and fifty

8 eighty-two thousand and ninety-four

9 nineteen thousand and nine

10 one hundred and sixty thousand four hundred and seven

11 six hundred and five thousand and thirty-six

12 two hundred and thirty thousand and five

Decimal number system

A

Million	Hundred thousand	Ten thousand	Thousand	Hundred	Ten	Unit
1 000 000	100 000	10 000	1000	100	10	1
$10 \times 10 \times 10 \times 10 \times 10 \times 10$	$10 \times 10 \times 10 \times 10 \times 10$	$10 \times 10 \times 10 \times 10$	$10 \times 10 \times 10$	10×10	10	1

1 million is 1000 thousands

Write in figures:

1 1 million   2 $\frac{1}{2}$ million   3 $\frac{1}{4}$ million   4 $\frac{3}{4}$ million   5 2.5 million.

Look at the table above. How many times greater is:

6 one thousand than one hundred   7 ten thousand than one hundred

8 one million than one hundred thousand   9 one million than one thousand?

B

These are estimated population figures.

Belfast	363 000
Birmingham	1 058 800
Coventry	338 860
Edinburgh	475 042
Glasgow	856 000
Leeds	746 000
Liverpool	539 700
Manchester	488 518
Motherwell	162 000
Norwich	121 688
Swansea	192 500
York	101 900

1 Read each estimate to your partner who will check from the answer book.

Which town or city has a population of:

2 more than 1 million

3 between $\frac{1}{2}$ million and 1 million

4 between $\frac{1}{4}$ million and $\frac{1}{2}$ million

5 less than 200 000

6 less than one hundred and ten thousand?

7 Write the names of the towns in order of size, putting the one with the largest population first.

8 Collect examples of large numbers. These may be obtained from Whitaker's Almanack, other reference books, encyclopaedias and newspapers, etc.

C

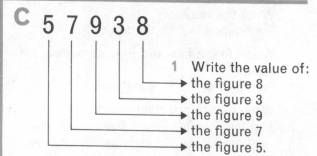

1 Write the value of:
→ the figure 8
→ the figure 3
→ the figure 9
→ the figure 7
→ the figure 5.

Write the value of each figure underlined.

2 5<u>2</u>6.4   3 93 <u>0</u>06   4 27 <u>9</u>16

5 81.<u>6</u>5   6 <u>23</u>0 950   7 38.8<u>6</u>

8 <u>5</u>43 871   9 873.<u>9</u>   10 <u>3</u> 051 807

Rearrange the figures below to make:

11 the largest possible number

12 the smallest possible number.

8	3	9	0	4	6

Multiply each of these numbers:

by 10   13 3974   14 250.5

        15 17.46   16 330.02

by 100. 17 36.9   18 9060

        19 78.43   20 26 875

Write the answer without a remainder when each of these numbers is divided:

by 10   21 409.3   22 3580

        23 5036   24 21 600

by 100. 25 30 409   26 760

        27 4016   28 6 253 900

Money

A The British money system is based on the **decimal number system** and for this reason is called a **decimal currency**.

£1·00	
£0·10	= **1 tenth** of £1·00 = 1 TEN
£0·01	= **1 hundredth** of £1·00 = 1p

When writing sums of money, the decimal point separates the whole £s from the fractions.

Look at this sum of money. **£34·57**

Write the value of:
1 the figure 4   2 the figure 3.

Write, first as £s and then as pence, the value of:
3 the figure 5   4 the figure 7.

Write as decimal fractions of £1:
5 30p   6 50p   7 60p   8 90p
9 8p   10 4p   11 9p   12 2p.

How many TENS have the same value as:
13 £0·20   14 £0·40   15 £0·70   16 £0·80
17 £1·30   18 £1·90   19 £3·60   20 £5·50?

How many pence have the same value as:
21 £0·06   22 £0·03   23 £0·05   24 £0·07
25 £0·25   26 £0·88   27 £1·49   28 £1·34?

B Write each total as £s.
1 £1, 7 TENS, 8p   2 £3, 2 TENS, 8p
3 £2 and 57p   4 £4 and 26p
5 £5 and 3p   6 £3 and 9½p
7 5 TENS and 5½p   8 37 TENS and 7p

Write and complete:
9 **£5·29** = £□, □ TENS, □p
= □ TENS, □p = □p

10 **£4·03** = £□, □ TENS, □p
= □ TENS, □p = □p

11 **759p** = £□, □ TENS, □p
= □ TENS, □p

12 **906p** = £□, □ TENS, □p
= □ TENS, □p

C Write the value of each figure underlined.
1 £1<u>3</u>0·62   2 £708·<u>5</u>0   3 £39·0<u>8</u>
4 £<u>2</u>0·15   5 £123·9<u>7</u>   6 £10·3<u>4</u>

Multiply by 10.
7 £1·63   8 £12·04   9 £0·75
10 £0·05   11 £1·40   12 £30·10

Multiply by 100.
13 £1·36   14 £0·58   15 £0·09
16 £10·02   17 £2·10   18 £5·71

Divide by 10.
19 £200·00   20 £37·50   21 £10·20
22 £56·00   23 £190·70   24 £306·00

Divide by 100.
25 £36·00   26 £198·00   27 £540·00
28 £10·00   29 £103·00   30 £700·00

Look at this sum of money.   W X Y Z
How many times is: **£33·33**
31 the 3 marked X greater than the 3 marked Y
32 the 3 marked W greater than the 3 marked Y
33 the 3 marked Z smaller than the 3 marked Y
34 the 3 marked Z smaller than the 3 marked X?

Write as £s the difference between:
35 £7·00 and £0·70   36 £80·80 and £8·08
37 £6·00 and £0·06   38 £32·00 and £0·32.

D Copy and complete this table by choosing the least number of notes and coins to make each total.

	total	notes			coins				
		£10	£5	£1	50p	10p	5p	2p	1p
1	£3·42								
2	£4·73								
3	£9·38								
4	£12·56								
5	£18·67								
6	£26·84								

Number and money addition practice

Number fact test Draw five columns **A, B, C, D** and **E**.
Number the columns from **1** to **8** as shown below.

Write the answers only. Try to beat the clock. Time: 3 minutes

	A	B	C	D	E
1	7+3	4+7	9+7	8+8	7+4
2	2+9	6+9	5+6	4+9	9+8
3	8+0	7+5	4+8	7+6	7+7
4	6+4	9+3	3+9	8+4	8+5
5	2+8	7+8	6+6	9+6	7+9
6	9+5	3+8	5+7	8+7	8+6
7	0+7	6+7	8+3	5+9	6+5
8	5+8	8+9	9+4	6+8	9+9

F Write the answers only.

1	5+78	7	47+7	13	35p+26p	19	68p+27p	25	77p+18p
2	9+55	8	79+9	14	29p+57p	20	23p+59p	26	69p+16p
3	6+77	9	88+6	15	34p+39p	21	67p+25p	27	36p+58p
4	6+49	10	19+2	16	45p+47p	22	39p+28p	28	55p+29p
5	7+36	11	26+6	17	28p+48p	23	17p+49p	29	38p+45p
6	8+89	12	38+4	18	37p+54p	24	58p+33p	30	44p+48p

G Write the answers only. Check each total by first adding up and then by adding down.

1	2	3	4	5
593	47.0	£	£	25 p
367	72.7	14·07	3·07	16 p
125	244.8	28·75	$0·52\frac{1}{2}$	$43\frac{1}{2}$p
86	5.5	32·46	$1·80\frac{1}{2}$	$16\frac{1}{2}$p
+ 49	+104.0	+17·39	+6·39	+49 p

6	7	8	9	10
13.08	1580	£	£	£
27.56	9304	250·55	19·56	3·16
28.50	6712	79·30	8·93	1·07
+ 6.96	+3406	8·94	36·06	0·88
		+ 0·79	+42·78	+2·65

H By adding across, find the total of each of the following in £s.
Check each total by adding across in the other direction.

1	$32\frac{1}{2}$p+14p+75p+$16\frac{1}{2}$p	2	43p+17p+$23\frac{1}{2}$p+$16\frac{1}{2}$p	3	26p+17p+54p+78p
4	65p+42p+$87\frac{1}{2}$p+50p	5	$9\frac{1}{2}$p+27p+52p+35p	6	29p+19p+$53\frac{1}{2}$p+48p
7	57p+22p+95p+$46\frac{1}{2}$p	8	18p+32p+48p+87p	9	$33\frac{1}{2}$p+7p+14p+63p

Number and money subtraction practice

Number fact test Draw five columns **A**, **B**, **C**, **D** and **E**.
Number the columns from **1** to **8** as shown below.

Write the answers only. Try to beat the clock. Time: 3 minutes

A	B	C	D	E
1 10−6	1 14−9	1 11−4	1 15−8	1 17−9
2 9−9	2 12−6	2 14−6	2 12−3	2 13−7
3 8−5	3 13−8	3 12−8	3 13−5	3 16−8
4 11−3	4 15−7	4 13−6	4 16−7	4 11−2
5 12−9	5 14−5	5 11−5	5 14−8	5 12−4
6 6−0	6 11−9	6 15−9	6 11−7	6 18−9
7 10−7	7 12−7	7 14−7	7 15−6	7 16−9
8 9−4	8 13−9	8 13−4	8 12−5	8 17−8

F Write the answers only.

1 40−6	7 32−7	13 41−27	19 77−48	25 86−27
2 50−8	8 67−9	14 72−53	20 61−12	26 53−15
3 90−2	9 51−6	15 84−18	21 55−27	27 92−44
4 60−11	10 42−5	16 95−39	22 44−16	28 31−18
5 80−23	11 76−8	17 62−26	23 82−58	29 75−36
6 70−35	12 93−4	18 53−28	24 91−34	30 66−29

G Find the change from:

a TEN after spending

1 $3\frac{1}{2}$p	5 $5\frac{1}{2}$p
2 $1\frac{1}{2}$p	6 $2\frac{1}{2}$p
3 $4\frac{1}{2}$p	7 $6\frac{1}{2}$p
4 $7\frac{1}{2}$p	8 $8\frac{1}{2}$p

a FIFTY after spending

9 16p	13 13p
10 39p	14 24p
11 42p	15 18p
12 27p	16 35p

a £1 note after spending

17 32p	21 69p
18 75p	22 44p
19 56p	23 23p
20 17p	24 61p.

H Write the answers only. Check each answer by adding.

1 307 −168	2 93.2 − 8.6	3 5007 −2398	4 4711 −3020	5 6520 −5291
6 £ 13·06 − 8·98	7 £ 27·80 − 8·71	8 £ 14·05 −10·08	9 £ 90·00 −14·91	10 £ 18·31 − 9·77

Set down and work the following. Check each answer by adding.

11 ten thousand−3072	12 £74−£50·30	13 £9·30−56p	14 £42·67−£23·70
15 £2·07−89p	16 £3·42−$69\frac{1}{2}$p	17 £10·10−£1·01	18 £201·45−£10·54

Number and money   addition, subtraction

A

Look at the coins above. Find the value of:

1 the FIFTIES
2 the TENS
3 the FIVES
4 the bronze coins.

5 Find the total value of the coins.

Find the sum of:

6 25 TWOS and 50 pennies
7 3 £5 notes and 16 FIFTIES
8 8 TENS, 5 FIVES and 8 TWOS
9 20 FIFTIES, 20 TWOS and 12 pennies

10 9 FIVES, 6 TWOS and 13 pennies
11 3 FIFTIES, 2 TENS and 7 FIVES
12 5 FIFTIES, 9 TENS and 6 FIVES
13 6 FIFTIES, 14 TENS and 9 TWOS.

B

1 Find the sum of money which is $93\frac{1}{2}$p less than £3·20.
2 Increase 756 by one quarter.
3 Increase £8·76 by one half.
4 Decrease 858 by one third.
5 Decrease £5·28 by one sixth.

Find the value of x in each of the following.

6 $107+x=320$
7 $x-87=225$

8 What must be added to £7·16 to make £10?

On a visit to the seaside, David spent £1·80 on bus fares, 94p for lunch, 55p for tea and 86p on amusements.

9 Find the total cost of the day's outing.
10 How much change was there from a £5 note?

There were 1274 people at a concert. 394 each paid 2 TENS and the rest 1 TEN each.

11 How many people paid 1 TEN?
12 Find the total amount of money paid for admission.

C

Genuine Bargains January Sale	usual price	sale price
socks, pair	58p	45p
shirts	£3·50	£2·95
pullovers	£4·20	£3·25
blazers	£8·15	£7·50
duffle-coats	£10·30	£8·90

1 Find by how much each article is reduced in the sale.
2 Mrs Grant bought 2 pairs of socks, a pullover and a blazer. How much did she save by buying at the sale?
3 How much did Mrs Brown pay for two shirts and a duffle-coat?

Slapton School Attendance for one week					
	Mon.	Tues.	Wed.	Thurs.	Fri.
class 1	23	24	26	22	25
class 2	18	23	17	20	19
class 3	25	25	22	28	26
class 4	18	17	18	19	16
class 5	15	13	17	19	16

Find:

4 the total attendance for each day
5 the grand total for the week
6 the total weekly attendance for each class
7 the grand total attendance for the classes.

If your answers to questions 5 and 7 are not the same, work questions 4 to 7 again.

Number and money addition, subtraction

A

1 Find the value of each letter.

$a+17=26$ $19+15=40-g$
$19+b=36$ $17+27+3=h$
$c-5=28$ $18-7=6+j$
$23-d=5$ $23-(8+7)=k$
$37=50-e$ $15+3=m+9$
$39=f+20$ $40-16=30-n$

How much change from a £1 note after buying:

2 $\frac{1}{2}$ kg of cheese at £1·80 per kg
3 $\frac{1}{2}$ kg of butter at £1·18 per kg
4 $1\frac{1}{2}$ kg of sugar at 30p per kg
5 $\frac{1}{4}$ kg of bacon at £1·30 per $\frac{1}{2}$ kg
6 4 eggs at 30p for $\frac{1}{2}$ dozen?

Find each missing amount.

	given in payment	amount spent	change
7	£2·00	£1·16	☐
8	4 TENS	☐	$7\frac{1}{2}$p
9	☐	56p	44p
10	a FIFTY	25p+16p	☐
11	3 £1notes	☐	73p
12	☐	£8·22	£1·78
13	3 FIFTIES	28p+74p	☐
14	£5 note	☐	£1·35
15	☐	43p+16p	41p
16	£1 note	13p+12p+8p	☐

B

1 By how much is £3·45 greater or less than 5 FIFTIES, 7 TENS and 9 FIVES?

2 By how many is six thousand greater than two thousand and ninety-eight?

3 Find the difference between 413 tenths and 413 hundredths.

4 What sum of money must be added to £13·60 to make £18·25?

5 Take the sum of 87, 39 and 103 from 500.

6 What number must be added three times to 31 to make 76?

Write and complete using the sign >, < or = in place of ●.

7 $37+39$ ● $113-38$ 8 80 ● $27+63$
9 $15+16$ ● $13+17$ 10 90 ● $150-56$
11 $y-17$ ● $17+y$ 12 £1 ● 15 FIVES

C

Alston Swimming Pool numbers paying for admission			
	June	July	increase (+) decrease (−)
men	1093	876	
women	1398	1507	
children	3029	4108	

1 Find the increase (+) or the decrease (−) in the number of men, women and children using the pool from June to July.

How many adults went to the pool during:
2 June   3 July?

How many more children than adults went to the pool in:
4 June   5 July?

At Christmas, Tim was given money instead of presents so that he could buy a Scout uniform. He made an account to show the money he received and spent.

money received		money spent	
	£		£
Father	4·50	beret	2·04
		shirt	5·15
Mother	2·75	trousers	8·10
Grandparents	7·80	belt	1·09
		neckerchief	0·43
Aunts and Uncles	5·62	woggle	0·15

6 How much did he receive?
7 How much did he spend on the uniform?
8 How much had he left?

Graphs

A Tim and Anne made a count of the cars which passed the school between 08.30 and 09.30, and the number of people in each car.

They made this graph to show the result.

What information is given on:

1 the vertical axis

2 the horizontal axis of the graph?

3 In how many of the cars was there the driver only?

4 Find the total number of cars counted.

5 What fraction of this total number of cars carried 4 people?

6 How many people travelled in all the cars?

7 How many buses each holding 50 people would be required to carry this number of people?

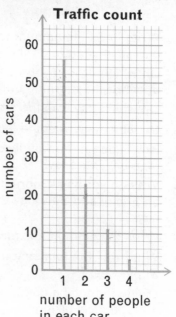

Traffic count

number of cars

number of people in each car

B The next day, Tim and Anne made a second count at the same time and place.

This is a copy of the record sheet they made.

number of people	number of cars
1	JHT JHT JHT JHT JHT JHT JHT JHT IIII
2	JHT JHT JHT JHT JHT II
3	JHT JHT IIII
4	JHT II

Find how many cars there were with these numbers of people:

1 1 person   2 2 people

3 3 people   4 4 people.

5 Draw a graph, using the same scale as the one above, to show the results of this count.

6 Compare the two graphs. What do you find?

C

1 Draw and complete this table.

number of people	number of cars		
	1st count	2nd count	totals
1			
2			
3			
4			

2 Choose a suitable scale for the vertical axis and draw a graph to show the totals.

By how many times is the number of cars carrying only the driver greater than the number carrying:

3 2 people   4 3 people   5 4 people?

Cars are banned from some town centres. Cars may be left on the outskirts and people travel to the centre by bus.

6 From the work you have done, can you find the reason for this?

Graphs

A

1 Write in £s the amount represented by one small square on the vertical scale.

2 On which day do you think the store was open for the morning only?

3 On which day was the most money taken?

4 On which day was the least money taken?

5 How much more was taken on Friday than on Thursday?

6 Why do you think more money was taken on Friday and Saturday than on other days?

7 Write the amount taken each day.

8 What was the total amount taken for the whole week?

9 Divide the total amount by 6 to find the average daily takings.

10 On which days were the daily takings above average?

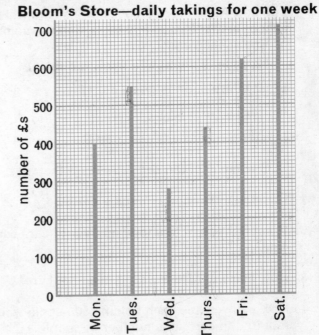

Bloom's Store—daily takings for one week

B

The graph shows the approximate distances in km from London by air to certain cities.

distances by air from London

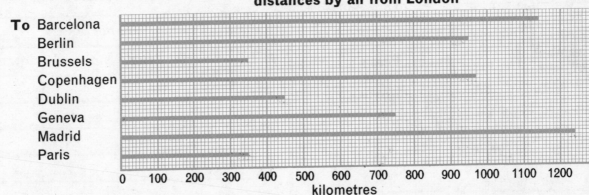

1 From an atlas, find in which country each city is situated.

By looking at the graph find:

2 which two cities are approximately the same distance from London

3 which journey is approximately twice the distance from London to Paris.

4 If the average speed of an aircraft is 700 km/h, which cities are within one hour's flying time from London?

5 Find the distance represented by one small division on the horizontal axis.

6 Find the approximate distance by air from London to each of the cities.

7 On squared paper, draw a graph to show the following approximate distances by air from London to the following.

Vienna	Amsterdam	Lisbon	Munich
1270 km	370 km	1560 km	940 km

Number and money multiplication practice

Place a strip of paper alongside each column in turn.
Write the answers only. Mark your answers and correct any mistakes.
Practise again and again until you can write the answers correctly and quickly.

A		B		C		D		E	
1	8×2	1	4×3	1	9×8	1	7×4	1	3×4
2	0×5	2	7×1	2	3×7	2	4×6	2	9×7
3	3×9	3	8×6	3	5×4	3	3×8	3	2×9
4	8×4	4	9×3	4	2×6	4	6×8	4	8×5
5	6×7	5	6×4	5	3×0	5	0×7	5	4×0
6	1×9	6	5×2	6	5×7	6	6×5	6	9×9
7	7×3	7	7×5	7	2×8	7	7×9	7	5×6
8	9×6	8	3×6	8	4×9	8	3×3	8	4×7
9	5×8	9	6×9	9	8×3	9	9×4	9	5×9
10	9×2	10	2×7	10	7×6	10	8×8	10	7×8
11	4×4	11	5×5	11	8×7	11	4×5	11	8×9
12	3×5	12	6×6	12	9×5	12	7×7	12	4×8

F Write the answers only.

1	(3×9)+8	6	(6×9)+7	11	(9×9)+7	16	(5×9)+6
2	(8×7)+5	7	(8×8)+6	12	(3×6)+5	17	(8×6)+4
3	(8×3)+2	8	(5×7)+6	13	(7×7)+3	18	(9×7)+5
4	(0×5)+4	9	(6×6)+5	14	(6×5)+4	19	(1×6)+5
5	(6×8)+3	10	(8×9)+8	15	(4×7)+6	20	(9×8)+4

G Write the answers only.

1	31−7(4)	5	33−5(6)	9	69−7(9)	13	46−6(7)	17	43−4(9)
2	19−9(2)	6	39−9(4)	10	35−8(4)	14	44−5(8)	18	45−7(6)
3	27−4(6)	7	37−4(8)	11	29−9(3)	15	59−9(6)	19	47−9(5)
4	60−7(8)	8	42−8(5)	12	38−7(5)	16	27−5(5)	20	23−7(3)

H Write the answers only.

1	504 ×2	2	705 ×8	3	£3·40 ×9	4	£1·86 ×7	5	£6·52 ×6
6	482 ×5	7	375 ×9	8	£0·77 ×4	9	£10·09 ×3	10	£8·64 ×7

11	19p×7	12	35p×8	13	76p×9	14	14p×6	15	$19\frac{1}{2}$p×5
16	$97\frac{1}{2}$p×2	17	17p×4	18	$4\frac{1}{2}$p×6	19	$23\frac{1}{2}$p×3	20	63p×7
21	55p×9	22	27p×3	23	46p×4	24	75p×5	25	55p×8

Multiply each of the following:

by 10	26	17.93	27	4.03	28	£21·50	29	£20·06	30	£31·02
by 100.	31	6.01	32	£89	33	£50·60	34	£4·03	35	£0·77

Number and money   division practice

Place a strip of paper alongside each column in turn.
Write the answers only. Mark your answers and correct any mistakes.
Practise again and again until you can write the answers correctly and quickly.

A		**B**		**C**		**D**		**E**	
1	$14 \div 2$	1	$25 \div 5$	1	$35 \div 5$	1	$16 \div 2$	1	$4 \div 4$
2	$90 \div 9$	2	$18 \div 6$	2	$24 \div 3$	2	$60 \div 6$	2	$30 \div 3$
3	$0 \div 3$	3	$56 \div 7$	3	$16 \div 8$	3	$30 \div 5$	3	$81 \div 9$
4	$36 \div 6$	4	$18 \div 9$	4	$12 \div 4$	4	$21 \div 7$	4	$35 \div 7$
5	$16 \div 4$	5	$0 \div 5$	5	$18 \div 3$	5	$15 \div 3$	5	$18 \div 2$
6	$24 \div 8$	6	$42 \div 6$	6	$48 \div 6$	6	$45 \div 9$	6	$72 \div 8$
7	$14 \div 7$	7	$8 \div 8$	7	$54 \div 9$	7	$24 \div 6$	7	$20 \div 5$
8	$27 \div 9$	8	$21 \div 3$	8	$0 \div 8$	8	$48 \div 8$	8	$27 \div 3$
9	$63 \div 7$	9	$36 \div 9$	9	$72 \div 9$	9	$63 \div 9$	9	$49 \div 7$
10	$28 \div 4$	10	$28 \div 7$	10	$42 \div 7$	10	$20 \div 4$	10	$30 \div 6$
11	$54 \div 6$	11	$40 \div 8$	11	$32 \div 8$	11	$64 \div 8$	11	$45 \div 5$
12	$56 \div 8$	12	$32 \div 4$	12	$24 \div 4$	12	$40 \div 5$	12	$36 \div 4$

F   Write the answers only.
Each answer includes a remainder.

Divide by 5:
1 47   2 39   3 48   4 98.

Divide by 7:
5 33   6 46   7 61   8 86.

Divide by 4:
9 19   10 31   11 38   12 66.

Divide by 8:
13 45   14 52   15 61   16 93.

Divide by 6:
17 22   18 41   19 53   20 82.

Divide by 9:
21 43   22 51   23 70   24 106.

Divide by 10:
25 48   26 59   27 86   28 117.

G   Find the value of each letter.

$23 = (5 \times a) + 3$ $19 = (2 \times e) + 5$ $27 = (5 \times i) + 2$ $20 = (2 \times n) + 4$

$14 = (2 \times b) + 2$ $39 = (f \times 9) + 3$ $21 = (j \times 2) + 3$ $30 = (7 \times p) + 2$

$28 = (c \times 3) + 4$ $67 = (8 \times g) + 3$ $32 = (3 \times k) + 5$ $18 = (3 \times r) + 3$

$33 = (5 \times d) + 3$ $50 = (6 \times h) + 2$ $47 = (5 \times m) + 2$ $52 = (s \times 7) + 3$

H   Write the answers only. Some examples have remainders.

1	$3)\overline{197}$	2	$5)\overline{375}$	3	$8)\overline{572}$	4	$6)\overline{744}$	5	$4)\overline{988}$
6	$3)\overline{2937}$	7	$9)\overline{2105}$	8	$7)\overline{4032}$	9	$8)\overline{5310}$	10	$6)\overline{4218}$
11	$5)\overline{3547}$	12	$4)\overline{4803}$	13	$9)\overline{1080}$	14	$7)\overline{1146}$	15	$8)\overline{2216}$

Work to $\frac{1}{2}$p.

16	$5)\overline{85p}$	17	$7)\overline{94\frac{1}{2}p}$	18	$9)\overline{76\frac{1}{2}p}$	19	$3)\overline{£0.25\frac{1}{2}}$	20	$8)\overline{£0.60}$
21	$6)\overline{£0.93}$	22	$4)\overline{£0.78}$	23	$2)\overline{£0.57}$	24	$5)\overline{£0.87\frac{1}{2}}$	25	$7)\overline{£3.04\frac{1}{2}}$
26	$9)\overline{£7.83}$	27	$8)\overline{£5.48}$	28	$3)\overline{£15.27}$	29	$6)\overline{£24.42}$	30	$4)\overline{£40.86}$

Number and money multiplication, division

A **Square numbers**

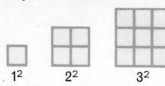

1^2 2^2 3^2 4^2

Write the value of these square numbers.

1   1^2 2 2^2 3 3^2 4 4^2 5 5^2

6   Write the next five square whole numbers to 10^2.

Cubic numbers

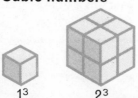

1^3 2^3 3^3

A short way of writing $2 \times 2 \times 2$ is 2^3 which is read as '2 cubed'.

Find the cubic number which is equal to:

7   $2^3 = 2 \times 2 \times 2$ 8 $3^3 = 3 \times 3 \times 3$.

Write each of the following in full and find the cubic number in each case.

9   4^3 10 5^3 11 6^3 12 7^3

Find the value of: 13 8^3 14 9^3 15 10^3.

B

1   Find the value of each letter.

$54 \div 9 = 36 \div a$ $\frac{1}{7}$ of $k = 209$

$63 \div 7 = 9 \times b$ $\frac{24}{6} = \frac{32}{z}$

$28 \div c = \frac{100}{25}$ $\frac{m}{9} = 37$

$\frac{162}{9} = 3 \times d$ $\frac{210}{n} = 7$

$\frac{168}{7} = e \times 8$ $\frac{p}{6} = \frac{1}{2}$

$8 \times 14 = 4 \times f$ $q(9) = 126$

$g \div 7 = 2.9$ $\frac{119}{r} = 7$

$h = \frac{1}{8}$ of 3408 $\frac{s}{7} = 178$

$56 \div 8 = j$ $\frac{378}{9} = t$

Divide by 10:

2   98.5   3   £2·45   4   5090   5   £35·00.

Divide by 100:

6   17   7   £6·00   8   8053   9   £209·00.

Write the set of factors of each of these numbers. Omit 1 and the number itself.

10   16   11   18   12   24   13   48   14   100

What is the largest possible remainder when a whole number is divided by:

15   6   16   8   17   9   18   27?

Write the product of:

19   6 and 56   20   7 and 19   21   8 and 47.

C

Find the cost of 10 articles if 1 costs:

1   27p   2 $43\frac{1}{2}$p   3   £1·48   4   £5·06.

Find the cost of 100 articles if 1 costs:

5   3p   6 $8\frac{1}{2}$p   7   £0·53   8   £1·10.

Find the cost of 1 article if 10 cost:

9   £34·00   10   £41·50   11   £2·25   12   £0·55.

Find the cost of 1 article if 100 cost:

13   £9·00   14   £50·00   15   £275   16   £17·50.

Find the cost of 1 article if:

17   4 cost £28·16   18   6 cost £10·50

19   8 cost £17·84   20   9 cost £55·62

21   3 cost $58\frac{1}{2}$p   22   7 cost $94\frac{1}{2}$p.

Find the cost of:

23   6 at 24p each   24   8 at £0·48 each

25   7 at £1·43 each   26   9 at £1·23 each

27   3 at £2·69 each   28   20 at £0·35 each.

Goods can be bought from shops by paying cash down or by paying **weekly** or **monthly instalments**.

	cash	instalments
calculator	£16·50	8 payments of £2·75
guitar	£68·70	10 payments of £8·25
bicycle	£75·45	6 payments of £16·15
radio	£43·18	9 payments of £5·70

29   Find the total paid for each item if payment is made by instalments.

30   By how much is it cheaper to pay cash for each item?

31   Give a reason why shops sell goods more cheaply for cash payments.

Measuring length

A

1 cm = 10 mm	1 mm = 0.1 cm

How many mm are there in:

1 4 cm   **2** 6 cm   **3** 8 cm   **4** 20 cm

5 25 cm   **6** 43 cm   **7** 62 cm   **8** 95cm?

How many cm are there in:

9 30 mm   **10** 50 mm   **11** 80 mm

12 100 mm   **13** 130 mm   **14** 290 mm

15 340 mm   **16** 570 mm?

Write as cm.

17 4 mm   **18** 7 mm   **19** 9 mm   **20** 2 mm

Write as mm.

21 0.5 cm   **22** 0.8 cm   **23** 0.6 cm   **24** 0.3 cm

Copy and complete:

25 11 mm = ☐ cm ☐ mm = ☐ cm

26 25 mm = ☐ cm ☐ mm = ☐ cm

27 46 mm = ☐ cm ☐ mm = ☐ cm

28 93 mm = ☐ cm ☐ mm = ☐ cm

29 108 mm = ☐ cm ☐ mm = ☐ cm

30 435 mm = ☐ cm ☐ mm = ☐ cm

31 647 mm = ☐ cm ☐ mm = ☐ cm.

How many mm are there in:

32 4.2 cm   **33** 8.7 cm   **34** 9.8 cm

35 7.1 cm   **36** 34.2 cm   **37** 64.6 cm

38 25.9 cm   **39** 33.4 cm   **40** 40.3 cm?

B

1 Measure these lines as accurately as possible.
Write the length of each   **a** in mm   **b** in cm.

W

X

Y

Z

Draw lines of the following lengths. Write the length of each in cm, as shown.

|←   14.3 cm   →|

2 5 cm 2 mm   **3** 78 mm   **4** 105 mm   **5** 20.3 cm   **6** 167 mm

In each of these shapes, find the following measurements in mm.

7 the square: each side, the perimeter, the diagonals

8 the rectangle: the length, the width, the perimeter, the diagonals

9 the triangle: the shortest side, the longest side, the perimeter

10 the circle: the radius, the diameter

C

To help you to make estimates, it is useful to know the length of your pace, your foot length and your span.

1 Mark and measure a distance of 10 paces. Then find the length of: **a** 1 pace in cm
b 3 paces in m   **c** 8 paces in m.

2 Mark and measure a distance of 10 foot lengths.
Then find the length to the nearest cm of:

3 1 foot length   **4** 6 foot lengths.

5 Mark and measure a distance of 10 spans. Then find the length in mm of:

6 1 span   **7** 4 spans   **8** 20 spans.

Measuring length

A

1 Make estimates of the measurements of many things in school, at home or out of doors, e.g. length and width of sheets of paper, books, tables, floors and lengths of corridors, playgrounds, etc.

2 To find the actual lengths, use the most suitable measure.

3 Keep a record of your work.

	estimate	actual measurement	error + or −

Estimating and measuring heights

4 Get a 2-metre rod or mark a height of 2 metres on the wall.
Compare a height of 2 metres with:
a your own height
b your teacher's height (your teacher will tell you this).

5 By how many cm is your height or your teacher's height greater or less than 2 m?

6 a Ask three of your friends to stand with their backs to the wall.

b Which of them is the shortest?
c Carefully mark this height on the wall.
d Measure the height to the nearest cm.
e Now estimate the height of each of the other two.
f Find each of their heights to the nearest cm.
Keep a record of your work.

7 First estimate and then measure the height of : a the radiator
b the cupboard c the blackboard.

B

It is difficult to measure the height of an object when its top is out of reach.
The picture shows a method of making a reasonable estimate using a 2-metre rod.

1 Compare the height of the rod with that of
a the tree b the building.
2 Estimate, in metres, the height of each.
3 Write a sentence telling how you found your answers.

C

1 Ask your partner to hold a 2-metre rod or a metre ruler upright near the side of the school building.
a Stand some distance away.
b Hold a pencil upright between your thumb and first finger.
c Stretch out your arm, close one eye and mark with your thumb the height of the rod or ruler as it appears on the pencil.
d Then, with your arm still outstretched, measure this distance into the height of the wall.

2 Write and complete:
The wall is approximately ☐ times as high as the ruler (or rod).
The estimated height is ☐ metres.

3 Find and try some of the methods used by Scouts and Guides for estimating heights.

4 Think of a method for finding the height of a high brick wall.
Describe the method you use.

Measuring mass

A The spring balances shown below are weighing machines.
For practical purposes they are commonly used to find the mass of articles.
You will learn more about mass and weight in Book 4.

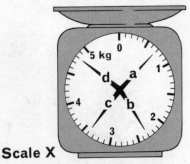

Scale X

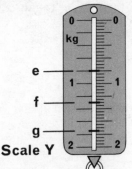

Scale Y

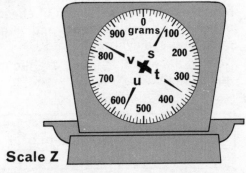

Scale Z

Spring balances of various kinds have different scales, on each of which a pointer shows the mass.

When using scales, find the mass each division represents.

Then learn to read accurately the recorded mass.

The pictures give some examples.

What is the maximum mass which can be recorded on:

1 scale **X**   2 scale **Y**?

3 On scale **X**, read the mass shown by each of the pointers **a**, **b**, **c** and **d**.

4 On scale **Y**, read the mass shown by each of the pointers **e**, **f** and **g**.

5 What is the maximum mass which can be recorded on scale **Z**?

6 What does one small division represent on the scale shown on the dial?

7 Read the mass shown by each of the pointers **s**, **t**, **u** and **v**.

What mass must be added to make:

8 pointer **s** read 250 g

9 pointer **t** read $\frac{1}{2}$ kg

10 pointer **u** read 750 g

11 pointer **v** read 1 kg?

B Write the following as kg and g, then as kg.

1 1250 g	2 3075 g	3 2480 g
4 750 g	5 5900 g	6 4060 g
7 1005 g	8 158 g	9 10 700 g

Write the following as grams.

10 0.9 kg	11 0.560 kg	12 3.180 kg
13 7.235 kg	14 2.015 kg	15 9.6 kg

Write and complete using the sign > or < in place of ●.

16 495 g ● $\frac{1}{2}$ kg   17 522 g ● $\frac{1}{2}$ kg

18 1010 g ● 1 kg   19 970 g ● 1 kg

Write each of the following to the nearest $\frac{1}{2}$ kg.

20 4400 g	21 2090 g	22 1810 g
23 3150 g	24 6340 g	25 2920 g

C Many goods at home and at school have the net mass printed on the packets.

1 Use some of these full packets and, without looking at the labels, estimate the mass of each.

2 Then find your error in each case.

3 Make a list of goods which are sold in packs of approximately $\frac{1}{2}$ kg.

4 Collect several articles, some heavy and some light. Estimate the mass of each.

5 Then use a spring balance to find the actual mass of each. Keep a record and show the error in each case.

6 Use the school scales to compare your own mass with that of your partner.

Measures

A

Work with a partner.

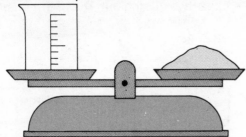

1. Get an empty litre measure and place it on one pan of a pair of scales.

2. Pour sand into the other pan until they balance.

3. Carefully fill the measure with 1 litre of water and then find in grams the mass of the water.

4. In the same way, find the mass of these amounts of water.
   - a half-litre (500 millilitres)
   - b 200 millilitres
   - c 100 millilitres

5. Use each of the three answers, **a, b** and **c** in turn, to find the mass of 1 litre of water.
   If you have worked accurately, you find that 1 litre of water has a mass of 1 kilogram.

6. Write and complete:
   1 litre of water has a mass of 1 kg
   □ml of water has a mass of 1000 g.

7. What is the mass of 1 ml of water?
   Find the mass of each of the following amounts of water.

8. 50 ml
9. 700 ml
10. 1.5 ℓ
11. $\frac{1}{4}$ ℓ
12. $\frac{3}{4}$ ℓ
13. 4.800 ℓ

14. A litre bottle filled with water has a mass of 1.570 kg.
    What is the mass of the empty bottle?

15. How much less than 2 kg is the mass of $1\frac{3}{4}$ litres of water?

16. An empty bottle has a mass of 280 g. 220 ml of water is poured into it. What is the total mass of the bottle and water?

17. An empty cask has a mass of 1.2 kg. When filled with water, it has a mass of 3.5 kg. How many ml does it hold?

B

Remember
A cube the sides of which measure 1 centimetre is called a **cubic centimetre** which is written **1 cm³**.

The picture shows a plastic box, the inside measurements of which are

10 cm long,
10 cm wide
and
10 cm high.

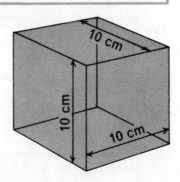

You will need a plastic box of this size to help you to make some important discoveries about the relationships between measures of

length, mass and **volume.**

1. Name the shape of the plastic box.

2. How many cubic centimetres will fit into one layer covering the bottom of the box?

3. How many of these layers will the box hold?

4. Find the total number of cm³ the box will hold.

5. Measure 1 litre of water carefully and pour it into the box.
   How much water does the box hold?

   Write and complete:

6. 1 litre of water has the same volume as □cm³

7. 1000 cm³ or □ml of water has a mass of □g

8. 1 cm³ or □ ml of water has a mass of □ g.

   Find:
   - a the volume in cm³
   - b the mass in g of

9. 600 ml
10. 150 ml
11. $1\frac{1}{4}$ ml of water.

Remember The mass of 1 ℓ or 1000 cm³ of water is 1 kg or 1000 g.

Measures

A Medicine bottles are provided in these sizes.

500 mℓ   300 mℓ   200 mℓ
150 mℓ   100 mℓ   50 mℓ

1 If a bottle of each size were filled with water, what would be the volume of the water in each bottle in cm³?

2 the mass of water in each bottle?

3 If the water from each bottle were poured into a 2 litre jug, what would be the mass of water in kg?

4 By how many mℓ would the jug be less than full?

> **Remember** A 5 mℓ medicine spoon is a useful measure.

5 If two 5 mℓ measures of medicine are taken four times a day, for how many days will 200 mℓ be sufficient?

6 Measure as accurately as you can the capacity, volume and mass of some small containers, e.g. teacups, egg-cups, fish paste jars, etc.

Make a chart and keep a record of your results.

	capacity mℓ	volume cm³	mass g
teacup			

7 Use measures to find the capacity of larger containers which you think hold a litre or more, e.g. bowls, basins, a bucket, etc. Find and record for each:
a the approximate capacity in ℓ
b the volume in cm³ **c** the mass in kg.

8 The liquid contents of bottles and tins are sometimes printed in mℓ on the labels. From such labels, find the quantities in which various liquids are usually sold.

B Copy and complete the following, then check the answers.

1 3297 mm = ☐ m ☐ mm = ☐ m
2 1037 m = ☐ km ☐ m = ☐ km
3 5500 g = ☐ kg ☐ g = ☐ kg
4 2250 mℓ = ☐ ℓ ☐ mℓ = ☐ ℓ

5 4.860 m = ☐ m ☐ mm = ☐ mm
6 3.080 km = ☐ km ☐ m = ☐ m
7 1.430 kg = ☐ kg ☐ g = ☐ g
8 2.565 ℓ = ☐ ℓ ☐ mℓ = ☐ mℓ

C Copy these tables and complete them by filling in the empty spaces.

1

mm	m
	1.987
3750	
	0.852
600	

2

m	km
2125	
	4.050
400	
	0.125

3

g	kg
	1.250
550	
	6.020
10	

4

mℓ	ℓ
2750	
	0.025
5	
	0.099

D Write the answers in kg.
1 1.650 kg × 4   **2** 375 g × 6
3 ½ kg + 870 g   **4** 2.7 kg + 456 g
5 2.430 kg − 750 g   **6** 14 kg ÷ 8

Write the answers in m.
7 175 cm × 4   **8** 1340 mm × 7
9 918 mm + 627 mm   **10** 4.670 m + 1550 mm
11 8 m − 2532 mm   **12** 4263 mm ÷ 3

Write to the nearest ½ kg.
13 4.760 kg   **14** 13.240 kg   **15** 560 g
16 5.80 kg   **17** 1150 g   **18** 2450 g

Write to the nearest litre.
19 7.470 ℓ   **20** 9.625 ℓ   **21** 6.075 ℓ

Write to the nearest m.
22 259 cm   **23** 1.450 m   **24** 3.180 m
25 4720 mm   **26** 3250 mm   **27** 5500 mm

Puzzle corner

A

Copy and complete the puzzle.

Across
2 $(2 \times 70) \div 4$
5 $600 \div 30$
6 $\frac{176}{2}$
7 0.57×100
8 $3 \times 3 \times 3$
9 $432 \div 8$
11 $4900 \div 49$
12 $1 + 0 + 9 + 8 + 15$

Down
1 $4 + 80 + 600 + 2000$
2 $4^2 + 16$
3 $(250 \times 2) \div 10$
4 $4000 - 2222$
8 $2 \times 20 \times 6$
9 $\frac{1}{8}$ of 400
10 $(9 \times 9) - 58$

B

1 Eleven posts were set in a straight row so that each post was 2.5 m from the next. Find the distance from the first to the last post.

2 Divide £1·35 between Peter, James and John so that Peter has one TEN more than James and James one TEN more than John.

3 Tom is 9 and his brother is 3. How old will Tom be when he is twice his brother's age?

4 Find the sum of the two largest prime numbers less than 50.

5 What is $\frac{1}{4}$ of $\frac{1}{2}$?

6 A mark is made 55 mm from one end of a metre rod and another mark 85 mm from the other end. How many cm apart are the two marks?

7 In a school there are 100 more girls than boys. There are 400 children in the school. How many boys are there?

8 A carton is twice as long, twice as wide and twice as high as another carton. How many of the smaller cartons are equal in size to the larger one?

C

This is the key to a secret code.

1	2	3	4	5	6
A	E	H	I	N	R

7	8	9	10	11	12
S	T	V	W	X	Y

1 Use the key to decode the following.
10 3 1 8   1 6 2
7 2 9 2 5 / 5 4 5 2 7?

2 Write the answer using the code.

Look carefully at the table. You see that each square number is equal to the sum of consecutive odd numbers.

$1^2 = 1 = 1$
$2^2 = 4 = 1 + 3$
$3^2 = 9 = 1 + 3 + 5$
$4^2 = 16 = 1 + 3 + 5 + 7$

3 What number when squared is equal to the sum of the first 7 odd numbers?

4 Write the consecutive odd numbers which equal 10^2.

In the example below, four 2s are used with different signs. Find the answers.

5 $2 + 2 + 2 + 2$
6 $(2 + 2 + 2) \times 2$
7 $2 \times 2 \times 2 \times 2$
8 $(2 \times 2) + (2 \times 2)$
9 $(2 \times 2) - \frac{2}{2}$
10 $2 + 2 + \frac{2}{2}$

Now use four 5s with different signs and set them out so that the answers are:

11 20   12 10   13 50   14 11
15 2   16 9   17 30   18 24.

Write the two numbers which come next in each of the following series.

19 10 000   1000   100   10   ☐   ☐
20 16   8   4   2   1   ☐   ☐
21 5   0   10   5   15   10   ☐   ☐
22 7.2   3.6   1.8   ☐   ☐
23 $\frac{1}{10}$ $1\frac{1}{5}$ $2\frac{3}{10}$ $3\frac{2}{5}$ ☐   ☐
24 2   6   4   8   6   10   ☐   ☐
25 1   2   2   4   3   6   4   8   ☐   ☐

Number and money $+$ $-$ $\times$ $\div$

A Write the answers only.

1 Find the total cost of 2 books, one costing 87p and the other 79p.

2 Find the cost of 6 books, each costing 98p.

3 Find the difference in price between a book costing £1·35 and one costing £0·83.

4 How many 9p notebooks can be bought for £1? How much money remains?

5 Steven read 19 pages on Monday and 47 pages on Tuesday. How many pages did he read during the two days?

6 There are 217 pages in Jane's book. She has read 129 pages. How many more has she to read?

7 Clare has 96 more pages to read. If she reads 8 pages each day, how long will it take her to finish the book?

8 48 seats were put into 6 equal rows. How many seats were there in each row?

9 There were 8 men, 7 women and 48 children in a bus. How many people was that altogether?

10 4 children bought a present costing £1·40. They each gave an equal amount. How much was that each?

11 Thomas paid a bill for £2·64 with a £5 note. What change did he receive?

12 Louise has 25p more than Elizabeth who has 19p. How much has Louise?

Paul spends 8p each day at school. How much does he spend at school

13 each week   14 in 10 weeks?

15 £6 is shared between 4 children. John's share is $\frac{1}{3}$, Sarah's is $\frac{1}{4}$, David's share $\frac{1}{6}$ and Helen has the remainder. How much is each child's share?

B

cornflakes 500 g 33½p
rice pudding RICE PUDDING 14p
coffee 100 g Roast Blend COFFEE £1·08
butter 30p ENGLISH BUTTER
yoghurt 9½p

1 From the prices above, find the total cost of one of each item.

2 What will be the change from 2 FIFTIES after buying 6 cartons of yoghurt?

3 A pack of 6 tins of rice pudding is on offer for 75p. How much is saved on each tin if a pack of 6 is purchased?

4 Name the coins, using as few as possible, given in change from a £1 note after buying a packet of cornflakes.

5 How many yoghurts can be bought for £1? Find the change.

6 How much must be added to a £1 note when buying 3 packets of cornflakes?

7 If 5 packets are bought, what will be the change from £2·00?

8 From the price given for the coffee, find the cost of   a 1 kg   b $\frac{1}{2}$ kg.

9 A 500 g jar of coffee can be bought for £4·95. How much cheaper is this for 100 g than that costing £1·08?

10 Which is the better buy per tin, and by how much, a pack of 10 tins of rice pudding costing £1·25, or the single tin at 14p?

11 If a 14p tin of rice pudding is shared between 4 children, what is the average cost for each child?

100 packets of butter have been purchased by the store for £25. If all the butter is sold, what will be

12 the total profit   13 the profit per packet?

Fractions

A

The strip above represents a whole one. It has been divided into equal parts.

What fraction of the strip is: **1** one part **2** the shaded part **3** the unshaded part?

> **Remember** In any fraction, the number below the line (the **denominator**) tells you into how many equal parts the whole one is divided.
>
> The number above the line (the **numerator**) tells you how many of the equal parts have been taken.

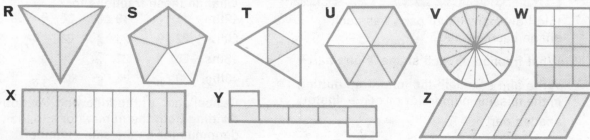

Each of the shapes **R, S, T, U, V, W, X, Y** and **Z** represents a whole one which has been divided into equal parts.

What fraction of each whole one is:

4 one of the parts

5 the shaded part

6 the unshaded part?

Copy and complete:

7 To find $\frac{5}{6}$ of a number or quantity, divide it into ☐ equal parts and take ☐ of the parts.

8 To find $\frac{3}{7}$ of a number or quantity, divide it into ☐ equal parts and take ☐ of the parts.

In the same way, describe how to find:

9 $\frac{3}{5}$ of 45

10 $\frac{9}{10}$ of $1\frac{1}{2}$ kg

11 $\frac{17}{100}$ of £1·00

12 $\frac{2}{3}$ of 24 litres.
Find the answer in each case.

13 Robert had 48 biscuits. He ate $\frac{3}{4}$ of them. How many biscuits had he left?

14 He gave away $\frac{2}{3}$ of the remainder. How many biscuits had he left?

Three men shared £91 so that Mr Sloane had $\frac{2}{7}$ of the money and Mr Cramp had $\frac{4}{7}$ of the money.

15 Mr Smith had the remainder. What fraction did he receive?

16 How much money did each man receive?

B Find:

1 $\frac{1}{2}$ of 97p

2 $\frac{1}{3}$ of 88.5 cm

3 $\frac{1}{10}$ of $2\frac{1}{2}$ kg

4 $\frac{1}{8}$ of 240

5 $\frac{3}{5}$ of 2.5 m

6 $\frac{2}{3}$ of 108

7 $\frac{5}{6}$ of 1 hour

8 $\frac{3}{4}$ of £2·60

9 $\frac{2}{9}$ of 882

10 $\frac{3}{10}$ of 1 litre

11 $\frac{4}{7}$ of 280

12 $\frac{7}{8}$ of 1 km

13 $\frac{7}{100}$ of £1·00

14 $\frac{19}{100}$ of £1·00

15 $\frac{3}{100}$ of £5·00

16 $\frac{7}{100}$ of £8·00

17 $\frac{7}{10}$ of 1 kg

18 $\frac{9}{10}$ of 1 litre

19 $\frac{2}{5}$ of $\frac{1}{2}$ kg

20 $\frac{2}{3}$ of $1\frac{1}{2}$ litres.

C Find the whole number or quantity when:

1 $\frac{1}{3}$ is $56\frac{1}{2}$p

2 $\frac{1}{5}$ is 250 g

3 $\frac{1}{10}$ is 33 mm

4 $\frac{3}{4}$ is 63p

5 $\frac{2}{3}$ is 96

6 $\frac{4}{5}$ is £3·00

7 $\frac{7}{10}$ is 1.4 m

8 $\frac{5}{8}$ is 62.5

9 $\frac{27}{100}$ is £0·27

10 $\frac{1}{9}$ is 45p

11 $\frac{5}{6}$ is 20 ℓ

12 $\frac{2}{7}$ is 14 g

13 $\frac{3}{4}$ is 60p

14 $\frac{7}{8}$ is 35 m

15 $\frac{3}{10}$ is 30 mm

16 $\frac{3}{8}$ is 18 km

17 $\frac{6}{7}$ is 24 g

18 $\frac{5}{9}$ is 45 mℓ

19 $\frac{3}{100}$ is 21p

20 $\frac{9}{100}$ is 36p.

Fractions

A Each of the shapes **W**, **X**, **Y** and **Z** represents a whole one which has been divided into equal parts.

W

X

Y

Z

1 Into how many equal parts has each shape been divided?

2 What fraction of each shape is one part?

Write and complete the following, putting in the missing numerator or denominator.

3 shaded part $\frac{1}{3} = \frac{\square}{6} = \frac{\square}{12} = \frac{\square}{24}$

4 unshaded part $\frac{2}{3} = \frac{4}{\square} = \frac{6}{\square} = \frac{16}{\square}$

5 In the same way, write and complete:
$\frac{8}{16} = \frac{\square}{8} = \frac{2}{\square} = \frac{\square}{2}.$

> **Remember**
> When the **numerator** and the **denominator** are both multiplied or divided by the same number, the value of the fraction is unchanged.

Write the following fractions, putting in the missing numerator or denominator in place of the letter **n** or **d**.

6 $\frac{2}{3} = \frac{n}{12}$ **7** $\frac{4}{5} = \frac{12}{d}$ **8** $\frac{5}{7} = \frac{n}{28}$

9 $\frac{7}{8} = \frac{21}{d}$ **10** $\frac{3}{4} = \frac{30}{d}$ **11** $\frac{7}{10} = \frac{n}{50}$

12 $\frac{2}{9} = \frac{20}{d}$ **13** $\frac{5}{6} = \frac{n}{30}$ **14** $\frac{3}{10} = \frac{n}{100}$

15 $\frac{2}{5} = \frac{40}{d}$ **16** $\frac{3}{4} = \frac{n}{100}$ **17** $\frac{19}{20} = \frac{95}{d}$

Change these fractions to:

12ths   **18** $\frac{1}{2}$ **19** $\frac{2}{3}$ **20** $\frac{3}{4}$ **21** $\frac{5}{6}$

20ths   **22** $\frac{1}{5}$ **23** $\frac{3}{5}$ **24** $\frac{7}{10}$ **25** $\frac{3}{4}$

18ths   **26** $\frac{2}{3}$ **27** $\frac{7}{9}$ **28** $\frac{1}{6}$ **29** $\frac{5}{6}$

40ths.   **30** $\frac{7}{8}$ **31** $\frac{3}{5}$ **32** $\frac{9}{10}$ **33** $\frac{3}{4}$

Cancel each of the following fractions by dividing both the numerator and the denominator by the same number. Make sure that each fraction is reduced to its **lowest terms**.

34 $\frac{3}{9}$ **35** $\frac{8}{14}$ **36** $\frac{4}{20}$ **37** $\frac{6}{10}$

38 $\frac{5}{25}$ **39** $\frac{12}{16}$ **40** $\frac{15}{25}$ **41** $\frac{16}{24}$

42 $\frac{14}{18}$ **43** $\frac{20}{30}$ **44** $\frac{18}{100}$ **45** $\frac{90}{100}$

46 $\frac{15}{100}$ **47** $\frac{24}{100}$ **48** $\frac{42}{100}$ **49** $\frac{25}{100}$

Try to find a rule which tells you when a number can be divided by:

50 2   **51** 3   **52** 4   **53** 5   **54** 10.

B Six whole centimetres are shown on the number line.

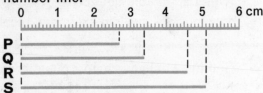

Each small division measures 1 mm which is $\frac{1}{10}$ of a centimetre.

The length of line **P** in tenths of cm is $\frac{27}{10}$ cm.

1 Write in tenths of cm the length of each of the lines **Q**, **R** and **S**.

Notice that in each of the fractions you have written, the numerator is greater than the denominator. Such fractions are called **improper fractions**.

The length of line **P** when written in cm is $2\frac{7}{10}$ cm. $2\frac{7}{10}$ is a **mixed number**.

Whole numbers with a fraction are called mixed numbers.

2 Write the length of each of the lines **Q**, **R** and **S** in cm as a mixed number.

3 Now write each of the lengths **P**, **Q**, **R** and **S** in cm as a decimal.

Write each of the following as an improper fraction:

as eighths   **4** $1\frac{1}{8}$ **5** $4\frac{3}{8}$ **6** $5\frac{5}{8}$

as sevenths.   **7** $2\frac{2}{7}$ **8** $3\frac{5}{7}$ **9** $6\frac{3}{7}$

Write each of the following as a mixed number.

10 $\frac{21}{5}$ **11** $\frac{37}{4}$ **12** $\frac{45}{8}$ **13** $\frac{32}{9}$

14 $\frac{23}{6}$ **15** $\frac{15}{7}$ **16** $\frac{31}{2}$ **17** $\frac{23}{5}$

Fractions

A Division by cancelling

Look at this example.

$$160 \div 25 = \frac{\overset{32}{\cancel{160}}}{\underset{5}{\cancel{25}}} = \frac{32}{5} = 6\frac{2}{5}$$

In the same way, work the following.

1	$90 \div 4$	2	$102 \div 14$	3	$200 \div 22$
4	$185 \div 15$	5	$165 \div 24$	6	$306 \div 16$
7	$393 \div 18$	8	$324 \div 16$	9	$153 \div 12$

Now work the following in the same way, and then write each answer to the nearest whole unit.

10 125 cm ÷ 15   11 £114 ÷ 12   12 140 kg ÷ 21

13 180 mℓ ÷ 25   14 119 ℓ ÷ 28   15 128 g ÷ 48

B

To add or subtract unlike fractions, change them to fractions with the same denominator.

Look at these examples.

a $\frac{3}{10} + \frac{1}{5} = \frac{3}{10} + \frac{2}{10} = \frac{5}{10} = \frac{1}{2}$

b $\frac{5}{8} - \frac{1}{4} = \frac{5}{8} - \frac{2}{8} = \frac{3}{8}$

Work the following.
Give each answer in its lowest terms.

1	$\frac{1}{6} + \frac{1}{3}$	9	$\frac{5}{6} + \frac{1}{12}$	17	$\frac{7}{12} + \frac{1}{6}$
2	$\frac{3}{8} + \frac{1}{4}$	10	$\frac{3}{5} + \frac{3}{10}$	18	$\frac{3}{20} + \frac{7}{10}$
3	$\frac{1}{2} + \frac{3}{10}$	11	$\frac{1}{8} + \frac{3}{4}$	19	$\frac{4}{5} + \frac{1}{10}$
4	$\frac{2}{5} + \frac{3}{10}$	12	$\frac{9}{16} + \frac{3}{8}$	20	$\frac{5}{8} + \frac{3}{16}$
5	$\frac{5}{6} - \frac{1}{3}$	13	$\frac{3}{4} - \frac{3}{8}$	21	$\frac{9}{10} - \frac{4}{5}$
6	$\frac{3}{5} - \frac{3}{10}$	14	$\frac{11}{12} - \frac{2}{3}$	22	$\frac{2}{3} - \frac{1}{2}$
7	$\frac{1}{2} - \frac{1}{6}$	15	$\frac{13}{16} - \frac{1}{4}$	23	$\frac{3}{4} - \frac{2}{3}$
8	$\frac{3}{8} - \frac{1}{4}$	16	$\frac{7}{8} - \frac{1}{2}$	24	$\frac{4}{5} - \frac{1}{2}$

Write in its lowest terms the fraction of these marbles which is:

25 striped   26 black   27 white.

C

Make sure your answers in sections **C** and **D** are in their lowest terms.

Find the fraction of the diagram which is:

1 coloured 2 black
3 white.

In a class of 32 children, 6 were absent.
What fraction of the class was:

4 absent   5 present?

Peter had a start of 7 m in a 100 metre race.
What fraction of the 100 m was:

6 the 7 metre start
7 the distance Peter actually ran?

The table shows each child's score out of 100.

What fraction of the total did each child have:

	score	possible score
Kevin	70	100
Alan	75	100
Jane	84	100
Sarah	76	100

8 right 9 wrong?

D

The pie chart shows how the children spent the 12 hours on a school journey.

What fraction of the total time was spent:

1 at the zoo
2 on meals
3 on the train   4 on the bus?

What fraction is:

5	50 min of 1 h	10	125 g of $\frac{1}{2}$ kg
6	30 kg of 100 kg	11	200 mℓ of $\frac{1}{2}$ ℓ
7	48 s of 1 min	12	18 mℓ of 90 mℓ
8	60p of £1·00	13	5 TENS of £2·50
9	40 cm of 1 m	14	750 g of 1 kg?

Fractions ratios

A

Two quantities can be compared by finding the relationship of the first to the second.
This relationship is called the ratio.

Five pounds is shared so that
Peter has £1 and Jane has £4.

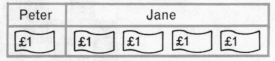

Peter	Jane
£1	£1 £1 £1 £1

Peter's share of the £5 is $\frac{1}{5}$.

The **ratio** of Peter's share to the £5 is
$\frac{1}{5}$ or 1:5 (this is read as '1 is to 5').

1 Write in two ways the ratio of Jane's
share to the £5.

The ratio of the £5 to Peter's share is
$\frac{5}{1}$ or 5:1 (this is read as '5 is to 1').

2 Write in two ways the ratio of the £5
to Jane's share.

4 children, in a class of 20, wore
spectacles.

Find, in its lowest terms, the fraction of
the children who

3 wore spectacles

4 did not wear spectacles.

5 Write each of the fractions as a ratio in
another way.

Write and complete:

6 One out of every □ children wore
spectacles.

7 □ out of every □ children did
not wear spectacles.

B

W   X   Y

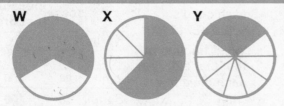

Write the fraction of each circle which is
1 shaded   2 unshaded.

For each of the circles, write in two ways
the ratio to the circle of:
3 the shaded part   4 the unshaded part.

For each of the circles, write in two ways
the ratio of the circle to the part which is:
5 shaded   6 unshaded.

In circle **W**, the ratio of the shaded part
to the unshaded part is $\frac{2}{1}$ or 2:1.

Write the following as ratios in two ways.
Circle **X**   7 shaded to unshaded
                8 unshaded to shaded

C

R _____

S _____

1 Measure, in cm, the length of line **R** and
line **S**.

2 What fraction is the length of line **R** to
the length of line **S**?

3 How many times longer is line **S** than
line **R**?

The ratio of line **R** to line **S** is shown as
a fraction in its lowest terms $\frac{R}{S} = \frac{1}{3}$
or as R:S=1:3.

4 Write in two ways, in its lowest terms,
the ratio of line **S** to line **R**.

T _____

5 Measure in cm the length of line **T**.
Write in two ways, in its lowest terms, the
ratio of:

6 line **S** to line **T**   7 line **T** to line **S**

8 line **R** to line **T**   9 line **T** to line **R**.

D

Remember Before quantities can be compared, the units must be of the same kind,
e.g. 10 cm to 1 metre = 10 cm to 100 cm = $\frac{10}{100} = \frac{1}{10}$ or 1:10.

Write in its lowest terms the ratio of the first quantity to the second.

1 25p to £1·50   2 1 mm to 5 cm   3 300 g to $1\frac{1}{2}$ kg   4 $4\frac{1}{2}$ kg to 6 kg   5 10 cm to 2 m

Making sure

A Turn to pages 7 and 8. Work sections **A** to **E** on both pages as quickly as possible. Mark the answers and correct any mistakes.

B First set down and then work the following.

1	£3·06+£1·59+£0·87	8	£10·67−£3·44	15	£2·46½×7	22	£23·08÷4
2	1079+65+834	9	10 000−866	16	1984×5	23	£14·43÷6
3	7026+44+550	10	56.87−0.98	17	£20·87½×6	24	2943÷9
4	79p+£1·48+£0·23	11	3050−350	18	20.16×2	25	10 110÷5
5	17.9+3.2+0.77	12	56.4−17.7	19	40 072×3	26	9107÷7
6	11+1.1+111	13	£3·55−£1·37	20	£0·54½×9	27	4264÷8
7	£1·16+£0·90+£1·77	14	9031−2222	21	30190×8	28	£28·71÷3

C A tradesman is paid his wages at the rate of £2·64 per hour.
How much is he paid for   1   2 hours   2   3 hours   3   5 hours   4   9 hours?

He is making a ready reckoner to help him to check his wages at the end of the week.

5   Copy and complete it.

hours	1	2	3	4	5	6	7	8	9	10	20	30	40
wages	£ 2·64	£	£	£	£	£	£	£	£	£	£	£	£

Using the ready reckoner, find his wages for:

6   15 hours   7   24 hours   8   37 hours   9   19 hours.

D

1   Ann had £5·00. She lost 3 coins. Now she has only £4·44. Name the coins she lost.

2   Decrease 514 by 87.

3   Increase £2·86 by 4 TENS.

How many quarters are there in:

4   $7\frac{1}{2}$ 5 $4\frac{3}{4}$ 6   15   7 $21\frac{1}{2}$?

Write and complete:

8   1063 = □tens □units = □units

9   9.18 = □tenths □hundredths.

Using the least number, name the notes and coins required to pay:

10   $73\frac{1}{2}$p   11   £0·39   12   £6·08   13   £10·87.

14   Find the total cost of:
5 kg at $15\frac{1}{2}$p per kg and
1 kg 200 g at 20p per $\frac{1}{2}$ kg.

15   Find the change from a £5 note after spending £1·36, £2·04 and 95p.

Write the value of each figure underlined.

16   10.86   17   30 760   18   6975   19   £18·64

E

1   Out of 15 examples, Joan had 9 right and Peter had 10. Write each child's score as a fraction in its lowest terms.

2   The amount of water in a measure was $\frac{1}{2}$ litre. When a jar was filled from the measure, 147 ml of water remained. What was the volume of the jar in cm³?

Look at the example below.
4579=4000+500+70+9
In the same way, write these numbers.

3   905   4   3048   5   20 167

Find the total of:

6   $(6×10^2)+(3×10)+(9×1)$

7   $(4×10^3)+(2×10^2)+(7×10)+(8×1)$.

8   A turkey has a mass of 7.5 kg.
Find its cost at 71p per kg.

Find the cost of:

9   4 m 50 cm at 37p per metre

10   1100 g at 15p per $\frac{1}{2}$ kg.

Time

A

morning
Y

afternoon
Z

1 Write the times shown on each clock face in words and then in figures.

Jane's bus leaves the bus stop at the time shown on clock **Y**.
It takes her 17 min to walk from home to the bus stop.

2 At what time must she leave home?

Father leaves for home at the time shown on clock **Z**, which is a quarter of an hour before his train departs.

3 At what time does the train depart?

4 The train journey takes 47 min.
At what time does the train arrive?

Write in words and then in figures the correct time if:

5 clock **Y** is   a   8 min slow   b   20 min fast

6 clock **Z** is   a   12 min slow   b   27 min fast.

B

1 Write the time shown on the clock face in figures and then in words.

p.m.

2 Find the number of min to the next hour.

3 How many h and min from the time shown to midnight?

Find the number of minutes to the next hour from:

4 2.15 a.m.   5   3.35 a.m.   6   8.28 a.m.

7 6.03 p.m.   8   10.11 p.m.   9   4.43 p.m.

10 What is the present time to a minute, shown by your own watch or by the school clock?

11 For how many h and min have you been at school today?

12 How long is it to the end of the school session?

C

How many h and min from:

1 7.37 a.m. to 11.15 a.m.

2 2.55 p.m. to 4.06 p.m.

3 11.35 a.m. to 4.15 p.m.

4   7.50 a.m. to 6.36 p.m.

5 10.00 p.m. to 5.40 a.m.

6   3.45 p.m. to 1.10 a.m.

7   8.06 a.m. to 2.30 p.m.?

Universal Trading Stores Business hours		
Mon.	8.30 a.m.	Thurs.	8.30 a.m.– 1.00 p.m.
Tues.	to	Fri.	8.30 a.m.– 6.00 p.m.
Wed.	12.45 p.m.	Sat.	8.30 a.m.– 4.00 p.m.

8 For how long do the Stores open on Wednesdays?

9 On which days do the Stores open in the mornings only?

10 For how much longer are the Stores open on Thursdays than on Wednesdays?

11 For how many h and min are the Stores open during one week?

D

Short periods of time are measured in seconds (s) or fractions of a second.

1 Using a stop-watch, work with a partner and find the time in seconds:
a   to run   b   to walk   c   to skip
a distance of 50 metres.

2 Consult a reference book and find the world record times for running:
a   100 m   b   200 m
c   400 m   d   1000 m.

Telephone charges are based on the duration of the call and the distance.
From a directory, find the charges for 'dialling direct from ordinary lines'.

Find the cost of a 6 minute call on a Monday at   a   10 a.m.   b   2 p.m.

3 for the local area

4 to a town 100 km away.

5 Find the shutter speeds on different kinds of cameras.

Time   Distance   Speed

A On the playing-field, Anthony walked in a straight line for one minute.
He marked and measured the distance in metres.
Then he made this chart to show the distances he could walk at this rate in 2 min, 3 min, 4 min, 5 min and 10 min.

time in min	1	2	3	4	5	10
distance in m	90					
distance in km	0.09					

1 Draw and complete the table.

At this rate, how many km could Anthony walk in:

2 20 min   3 30 min   4 40 min
5 50 min   6 15 min   7 60 min?

> Speed is often measured in **kilometres per hour** which is written for short as **km/h**.

8 Write Anthony's walking speed in km/h.
Anthony can walk 90 m in 1 min.

9 Is it always true to say that he can walk 180 m in 2 min, 270 m in 3 min and so on? Give a reason for your answer.

10 Using the method shown above, find your own walking speed, for a short distance, in km/h.

B

1 A good swimmer can swim 100 m in 1 min. Find this speed in km/h.

2 A champion athlete can run 100 m in 10 s. How many km/h is this speed?

3 A cyclist travelled at the rate of 30 km/h. How many min did it take him to cycle 1 km?

A car travels at 60 km/h. At this speed, how far will it travel in:

4 1 min   5 8 min   6 $\frac{3}{4}$ h?

7 A truck travelled 90 km in $1\frac{1}{2}$ h. Find its average speed in km/h.

8 An aircraft travelled 5040 km in 6h. Find its average speed in:
a km/h   b km per min (km/min).

C The diagram shows how certain towns or cities are connected by main roads.

Name the town or city on the diagram which is most

1 northerly

2 southerly

3 easterly

4 westerly.

5 A car travelling at an average speed of 68 km/h takes 4 hours to complete the journey from Inverness to Glasgow. Find the total distance in km.

6 The car took 2 hours to travel the 151 km between Glasgow and Carlisle. What was the car's average speed in km/h?

7 The average speed of a large truck was 35 km/h.
How long did it take for the journey of 140 km from Carlisle to Preston?

8 On a journey from London to Preston via Birmingham, a motorist took $4\frac{1}{2}$ h at an average speed of 78 km/h. Find the distance he travelled.

9 A motorist left his home in Doncaster at 10.00 a.m. to travel to London, a distance of 260 km.
He reckoned he could average 80 km/h. At what time would he arrive in London?

10 The distance shown on the odometer of a car for a journey from Inverness to Doncaster was 603 km.
The time taken was 10 hours.
Find the exact average speed of the car.

Time 24-hour clock

A Most timetables use the 24-hour clock to show arrival and departure times.

> **Remember** 24-hour clock times are written using four figures,
> the first two for hours, and the last two for minutes.
> A point usually separates the hours from the minutes.
> e.g. 07.45 is 7.45 a.m.   13.20 is 1.20 p.m.

Write these times as 24-hour clock times.

1 7.00 a.m.   2 8.17 a.m.   3 6.08 a.m.
4 1.54 p.m.   5 11.28 p.m.   6 noon

Write these times as 12-hour clock times.

7 02.55   8 18.12   9 13.27   10 05.30
11 15.45   12 11.19   13 23.10   14 00.15

B Look at the rail timetable.

London (Victoria)
Ashtead
Leatherhead
Bookham

Victoria	Ashtead	Leatherhead	Bookham
15.06	15.46	15.50	15.54
16.02	16.46	16.50	16.54
16.35	17.21	17.25	17.29
17.00	17.46	17.51	17.56
17.25	18.06	18.10	18.15
17.45	18.31	18.35	18.39

Write in 12-hour clock times the departure times from:

1 Victoria to Bookham
2 Ashtead to Bookham.

Find the time taken for these journeys.

3 Victoria to Leatherhead   dep. 16.35
4 Ashtead to Bookham   dep. 16.46
5 Victoria to Ashtead   dep. 17.45

A train arrives at Bookham at 17.56.
At what time did it leave

6 Victoria   7 Ashtead?

Which train leaves Victoria to arrive at Bookham within a few minutes of:

8 4.00 p.m.   9 5.00 p.m.   10 6.00 p.m.?

Which of the trains from Victoria to Bookham is:

11 the fastest   12 the slowest?

C

1 Study the timetable and then follow the journey on a map.

Sealink
London—Paris—London

07.55 dep.	London (Victoria)	arr. 18.39
09.08 arr. 10.00 dep.	Newhaven Harbour	dep. 17.26 arr. 16.45
14.00 arr. 14.50 dep.	Dieppe Maritime	dep. 12.45 arr. 12.16
17.12 arr.	Paris (St. Lazare)	dep. 09.45

2 Write the names of the two ports.

Find how long it takes to travel by train:
3 from London to Newhaven
4 from Dieppe to Paris.

5 Which journey takes less time, and by how many minutes, the journey from Dieppe to Paris or the return journey from Paris to Dieppe?

What time is taken on the Channel crossing:
6 on the outward journey
7 on the return journey?

8 A man left London at 07.55 for Paris and arrived back at 18.39 the next day. How long did he spend in Paris?

9 Which journey takes longer, and by how many minutes, the journey from London to Paris or the journey from Paris to London?

Time the calendar

A

How many days are there in each of these months:

1 June 2 Aug. 3 March 4 Sept?

Write the names of the following months and the number of days in each.

5 the 4th month   6 the 10th month

7 the 1st month   8 the 12th month

How many days are there in:

9 the last three months of this year

10 the first three months of next year?

Get a calendar for the present year. Find from it on which day is:

11 Christmas Day   12 New Year's Day

13 28th February   14 6th October

15 19th May   16 the last day in June.

17 If the first of July is on a Thursday, what are the dates of all the Sundays in July?

18 If September 30th is on a Thursday, what are the dates of all the Wednesdays in September?

19 Julie begins a fortnight's holiday on the 19th June. On what date does she return?

B

name	date of birth		
Joan	25	11	1972
Roger	30	9	1969
Ann	27	3	1974
Derek	29	10	1977

1 Write the names of the children in the order of their ages. Put the youngest first.

By how many years and months is:

2 Roger older or younger than Joan

3 Derek older or younger than Ann?

4 Find the age of each of the four children, in years and months, on 31st Dec. 1990.

5 What will be your age, in years and completed months, on 31st Dec. 2000?

Find the number of days, not counting the first day, from:

6 7th May to 15th May

7 19th Jan. to 8th Feb.

How many days **inclusive** from:

8 8th Sept. to 21st Oct.

9 30th October to Christmas Eve?

C

1 Christian people number the years from the Birth of Christ, but some religions number the years differently. Find how Jews and Moslems number their years.

The time line shows how the years are numbered in centuries from the **Birth of Christ**.

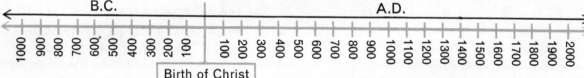

2 Find the meaning of B.C. and A.D.

When writing years before the birth of Christ, **B.C.** is written **after** the date, e.g. 55 B.C.

When writing years after the birth of Christ, **A.D.** is written **before** the date, e.g. A.D. 1066.

Below are the dates of two important world events in history:

the founding of Rome (753 B.C.) and the murder of Julius Caesar (44 B.C.).

3 How many years between these two dates?

The second World War ended in A.D. 1945, which is in the 20th century A.D.

In which century, A.D. or B.C., did these events take place in British history:

4 invasion by Julius Caesar, 55 B.C.

5 occupation by the Romans, A.D. 43

6 defeat of the Spanish Armada, A.D. 1588?

7 Find in a library book a list of important dates in world history.

8 Write in which century each took place.

9 Find the number of years between two of them.

Round numbers approximations

A

When exact accuracy is unnecessary, large numbers are often 'rounded off' to give an approximation to the nearest 10, to the nearest 100 or to the nearest 1000.

Rounding off to the nearest ten

If there is half 10 or more, count the next ten.

If there is less than half 10, no change is made to the tens.

Example As 6 is more than half 10, it is counted as 1 more ten.

28|6 **290** is the approximation.

1 Write 253 to the nearest 10.

Write these numbers to the nearest 10.
2 88 3 161 4 455 5 699 6 973

B

The table shows the number of children who attended a library during each of the first six months of the year.

Jan.	937	April	1650
Feb.	1284	May	1896
Mar.	1307	June	2120

To make a graph, the numbers are 'rounded off' **to the nearest hundred** in the following way.

9|37 As 37 is less than half 100, no change is made to the hundreds.

900 is the approximation.

12|84 As 84 is more than half 100, it is counted as 1 more hundred.

1300 is the approximation.

1 Round off, to the nearest 100, the numbers from the table for March, April, May and June. Check your answers.

monthly library attendances

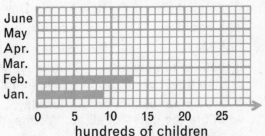

Look at the horizontal axis on the graph.
2 What does one small division represent?
3 Copy the graph and complete it for the first six months of the year.

Find for the six months:
4 the approximate total of attendances
5 the actual total of attendances
6 the difference between the two totals.

Write these numbers to the nearest 100.
7 4050   8 1973   9 3045   10 8064

C

The attendances at two football matches are given in this newspaper cutting.

Football Results Friendly matches

Everton 1   **Celtic 1**
          Attendance 49 000

Motherwell 2   **Burnley 2**
          Attendance 28 000

The exact number of spectators was 48 862 and 28 150 respectively.

The reported attendances are approximations to the nearest 1000.

These are made in the following way.

48|862 As 862 is more than half 1000, it is counted as one more thousand.

49 000 is the approximation.

28|150 As 150 is less than half 1000, no change is made to the thousands.

28 000 is the approximation.

Write these numbers to the nearest 1000.
1 9087   2 16 503   3 29 700
4 14 008   5 10 390   6 64 500
7 764   8 100 228   9 209 903

Round numbers approximations

A

| cm | 1 | 2 | 3 | 4 | 5 | 6 | 7 | 8 | 9 | 10 | 11 | 12 | 13 | 14 | 15 | 16 |
| mm | 10 | 20 | 30 | 40 | 50 | 60 | 70 | 80 | 90 | 100 | 110 | 120 | 130 | 140 | 150 | 16 |

W
X
Y
Z

Write the length of each of the lines
W, X, Y and **Z**: **1** in mm **2** in cm.

3 Now write the length of each line to the nearest cm.

Write each of the following to the nearest cm.

4	9.4 cm	8	15.1 cm	12	372 mm
5	20.7 cm	9	59.3 cm	13	115 mm
6	39.8 cm	10	69 mm	14	703 mm
7	50.5 cm	11	45 mm	15	194 mm

Write each of the following to the nearest metre.

16	3 m 79 cm	22	10.5 m	28	9 m 350 mm
17	8 m 50 cm	23	3.2 m	29	7 m 875 mm
18	10 m 16 cm	24	7.6 m	30	3 m 135 mm
19	6 m 5 cm	25	8.3 m	31	6 m 670 mm
20	9 m 28 cm	26	4.75 m	32	995 mm
21	2 m 61 cm	27	8.25 m	33	4 m 295 mm

B

	Write to the nearest km.		Write to the nearest litre.
1	2 km 800 m	13	3 ℓ 70 mℓ
2	6 km 500 m	14	8 ℓ 500 mℓ
3	9.9 km	15	5.985 ℓ
4	15.255 km	16	17.135 ℓ
5	19.5 km	17	10.830 ℓ
6	21.270 km	18	7.4 ℓ

	Write to the nearest kg.		Write to the nearest £.
7	5 kg 200 g	19	£1·80
8	10 kg 750 g	20	£4·12
9	7.050 kg	21	£7·50
10	0.975 kg	22	£5·28
11	1.495 kg	23	£0·89
12	8.710 kg	24	£2·06

Round off to the nearest whole unit.

25	57.6	30	$43\frac{1}{7}$	35	$9\frac{3}{5}$
26	139.5	31	$30\frac{1}{2}$	36	$20\frac{1}{6}$
27	29.28	32	$6\frac{3}{4}$	37	$28\frac{3}{10}$
28	609.8	33	$18\frac{1}{3}$	38	$15\frac{5}{12}$
29	25.07	34	$4\frac{7}{8}$	39	$19\frac{77}{100}$

C

Round off the following to the nearest whole unit.

1	$46\frac{1}{2}$p	5	£10·51	9	99.650 ℓ
2	£9·52	6	92.3 cm	10	309.85 m
3	70 cm 5 mm	7	5 km 45 m	11	5.376 m
4	3.875 km	8	16.050 kg	12	£102·09

By rounding off numbers to the nearest unit, you can find approximate answers which provide a useful check to many calculations.

Write an approximate answer to each of the following:

13 £9·87+£24·23+£17·08+£59·86

14 from 8 m take 4 m 196 mm

15 add 5 ℓ 126 mℓ to 7 ℓ 874 mℓ

16	£58·23−£39·90	22	5.210 kg ×7
17	£150·45−£48·17	23	9.923 ℓ ×9
18	$2\frac{1}{4}+5\frac{3}{8}+8\frac{1}{2}$	24	£9·75×8
19	$5\frac{1}{2}+2\frac{1}{6}+3\frac{1}{3}$	25	£6·13×6
20	$100−9\frac{7}{10}$	26	41.545 m ÷7
21	$58\frac{5}{6}−23\frac{1}{2}$	27	£19·80 ÷5.

28 Find the correct answer to each, and then find the difference between the correct and approximate answers.

Measuring temperature

A Get a Celsius thermometer which is used for taking air temperatures.

Make sure that you can read temperatures accurately from it.

Work the rest of this section with a partner who can check the answers.

Find the temperature of the air in:

1 the class-room   2 a corridor

3 the school hall.

4 What is the difference between the highest and the lowest of these temperatures?

5 Go into the playground and find the outside temperature.

6 Find the difference between the class-room temperature and the outside temperature.

7 Find the difference between the outside temperatures in the sun and in the shade.

Find the temperature of:

8 water as it comes from the cold tap

9 warm water in which you can wash yourself.

10 What is the difference in °C between the two temperatures?

B The diagram shows the **Celsius thermometer** scale which was introduced in the eighteenth century by a Swedish astronomer of that name.

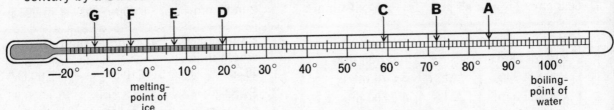

Look at the scale.
Write the temperature at which:

1 water freezes   2 water boils.

3 How many degrees are there between the freezing-point and the boiling-point of water?

4 How many degrees on the thermometer scale does each small division represent?

> Temperatures below freezing-point on the Celsius scale are shown by placing a minus sign (−) before the number of degrees registered. e.g. 5° below freezing-point is written −5°C.

How many degrees below freezing-point is each of these temperatures?

5 −3°C   6 −12°C   7 −20°C

8 What is a the highest b the lowest temperature which can be measured on this thermometer?

9 Read the temperature at each of the points marked **A, B, C, D, E, F** and **G**.

By how many degrees does the temperature **rise** or **fall** from:

10 **B** to **D**   11 **C** to **A**   12 **A** to **E**

13 **E** to **F**   14 **G** to **C**   15 **B** to **F**?

The air temperature at 09.00 is −2°C.
Find the temperature:

16 at noon if it has risen by 7°C

17 at 21.00 if it falls by 11°C from midday.

18 The freezing-point of mercury is −39°C. Write the reason why mercury is frequently used in thermometer tubes.

Find from a reference book:

19 the melting-point of lead and of iron

20 the temperatures at which three liquids, other than water, freeze.

Measuring temperature

A Temperatures are frequently shown on a graph so that the rise and fall can be seen easily.

The graph below shows the outside temperatures taken at 14.00 every day for five days.

Each thermometer reading is shown by a dot.

temperatures taken at 14.00

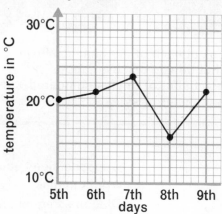

Answer these questions from the graph.

On which day was:

1 the highest temperature recorded

2 the lowest temperature recorded?

3 During which of these months, February, June, September were the temperatures taken?

Between which following days was there

4 the greatest fall in temperature

5 the sharpest rise in temperature?

6 Draw the table below and write in the temperature shown on the graph for each day.

5th	6th	7th	8th	9th

Copy and complete the following.

7 During the week the temperature at 14.00 varied between □°C and □°C.

The difference between these two temperatures is called the **range**.

8 Find the temperature range for the week.

9 Find the average temperature at 14.00 for the five days by:

a adding the temperatures

b dividing the total by the number of days.

10 On which days was the temperature at 14.00: above the average 11 below the average?

Find the range and the average of the following temperatures.

12	13°C	18°C	21°C	9°C	9°C
13	1°C	0°C	5°C	0°C	4°C
14	4°C	3°C	2°C	−1°C	
15	0°C	5°C	−2°C		
16	5°C	−3°C	3°C	−1°C	1°C

17 Record the outside temperatures on ten consecutive days taken at:
a 09.00   b 15.00.

18 Use these temperatures to draw two graphs.

19 From each, find the temperature range.

20 From each, find the average temperature to the nearest degree for the ten days.

B

The temperature in the rooms of a house with central heating can be controlled by an instrument called a **thermostat**.

1 What is the range of temperature shown on this picture of a room thermostat?

2 Give the reason why the temperatures on the scale do not exceed 25°C or go below 5°C.

3 At what temperature is the thermostat set?

4 Thermostats are also used to control temperature in water-heaters and the ovens in cookers.
Find out all you can about these and the range of temperatures at which they can be set.

Shapes

A Shapes are usually put into sets according to the number of sides they have.

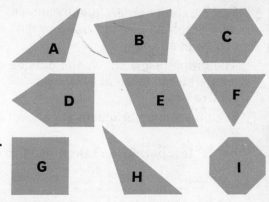

All shapes with straight sides are called polygons. ('poly' means many, 'gons' means corners)

Polygons with 3 sides are called triangles. ('tri' means three—three angles)

Polygons with 4 sides are called quadrilaterals. ('quad' means four, 'laterals' means sides)

1 Which of the shapes in this section are members of the following sets?

Q = {quadrilaterals}
T = {triangles}
M = {shapes with more than 4 sides}

2 Look at each of the shapes above. What do you discover about the number of angles compared with the number of sides?

B **Remember**

Square

4 equal sides
4 right angles
Diagonals equal and bisect each other
4 lines of symmetry

Rhombus

4 equal sides
Opposite sides parallel
Angles not right angles
Diagonals not equal but bisect each other
2 lines of symmetry

Rectangle

Opposite sides equal
4 right angles
Diagonals equal and bisect each other
2 lines of symmetry

Parallelogram

Opposite sides equal and parallel
Angles not right angles
Diagonals not equal but bisect each other
No lines of symmetry

1 Use a ruler and a set square to find which of the quadrilaterals below belong to each of the following sets.

S = {squares}   R = {rectangles}   H = {rhombuses}   P = {parallelograms}

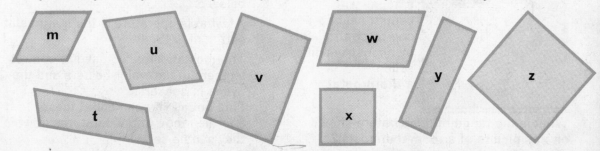

Shapes quadrilaterals

A

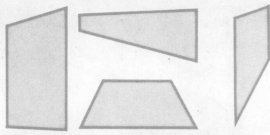

The quadrilaterals above do not belong to the sets of the quadrilaterals you have learned about, i.e. square, rectangle, rhombus, parallelogram.

The drawings are of quadrilaterals which are called **trapeziums**.

1 Using your ruler and set square, find:
   a how many angles in a trapezium can be right angles
   b how many pairs of parallel sides there are in a trapezium.

2 What can you find about the lengths of the parallel sides in a trapezium?

3 If the parallel sides were equal in length what would the shape be called?

4 Draw three trapeziums of different shapes and sizes. Measure their diagonals. What do you find in each case?

C

You know that the angles of a square or rectangle together make 4 right angles.

You can also discover how many right angles are made by the four angles of **any** quadrilateral.

1 On a piece of gummed paper draw a large quadrilateral of any shape.

2 Cut out the quadrilateral.

3 Mark the angles 1, 2, 3 and 4 as shown in the diagram.

4 Tear off each of the angles, fit them together and stick them on paper.

5 Now draw a rhombus, a parallelogram and a trapezium.

6 Repeat questions **2**, **3** and **4** with each shape. See if you get the same results each time.

7 Write and complete:
   the four angles of any quadrilateral together equal □° or □ right angles.

B

1 Which of the quadrilaterals below are members of the set T={trapeziums}?

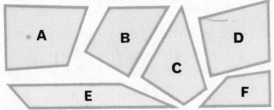

2 Three of the quadrilaterals do not belong to any of the special sets you have learned about. Which are they?
   In each of these three quadrilaterals, what do you notice about:

3 the lengths of the sides

4 the sizes of the angles?

5 Are any pairs of opposite sides parallel?

D

1 Measure the square and draw it on stiff paper.

2 Draw the diagonals and cut out the four triangles.

Using the four triangles each time, arrange them to make:

3 a rectangle   4 a parallelogram

5 a trapezium   6 a right-angled triangle.

7 Make a drawing of each shape and underneath write the name of each.

8 What is the area in cm² of each of the shapes you have drawn?

Puzzle corner

A Jane asked Susan to choose any number from this set.

$\{5, 10, 15, 20, 25, 30, 35, 40\}$

She then asked Susan three questions to find the chosen number.

Here are the questions and the answers.
Is the number an odd number?   No.
Is the number greater than 25?   Yes.
Is the number 40?   No.

1 What was the chosen number?

2 Ask your partner to choose one of the numbers. Then find the number chosen by asking three questions of your own.

Copy and complete:

3
```
  6 □
× □
─────
3 2 5
```

4
```
  8 □ 7
×   □
───────
4 8 4 2
```

5
```
  □ 4 6
×   □
───────
2 7 3 0
```

6
```
  4 2 □
×     9
───────
□ □ □ 6
```

B These clock faces are shown as seen in a mirror.
Write the time given on each clock.

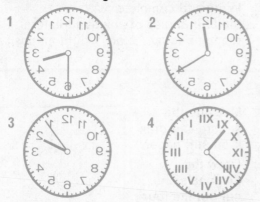

1   2

3   4

In the example below, the figure 8 is used five times and the answer is 10.

$\frac{88}{8} - \frac{8}{8} = 10$

5 Find a way to use the figure 8 seven times to make the answer 100.

Write the answers only.

6 $(5+5)-5$ 7 $(5+5)-5+(5-5)$

8 $(5\times5)-5-(5-5)$ 9 $5^2-(4^2+1^2)$

10 $8\times(8-8)$ 11 $(8+8)-(8+8)$

12 $(8\times8)\div(8\div8)$ 13 8^2-8

C

1 Trace and cut out each of the four quadrilaterals above.

2 Now fit them together to make a square. Stick the square on paper.

Nicola started to walk from her house to meet Steven at a rate of 7 km/h.

Nicola   6 km   Steven

Steven started to walk from his house to meet Nicola at a rate of 4 km/h.

3 How many metres apart were they after 30 minutes?

D

1 What is the greatest number which will divide into both 63 and 79 and leave a remainder of 7 in each case?

2 Find the value of both x and y.
```
      6 rem. x
6)xy
    x6
   ───
    x
```

Write the answers only.

3 $(75\times48)-(65\times48)$ 4 $\frac{8}{8}+\frac{14}{7}-\frac{4}{2}$

5 The difference between $\frac{1}{7}$ and $\frac{1}{8}$ of a number is 1. What is the number?

6 What date is the middle day of May?

7 What is the smallest number which will divide by 2, 3 and 4 and leave a remainder of 1 in each case?

8 Divide a mass of 1 kg into 2 parts, so that 1 part has a mass 3 times that of the other.

Four rules

A
Write the answers only.

1. $37+58+73$
2. $200-46$
3. $10\frac{1}{2}p+35\frac{1}{2}p+69\frac{1}{2}p$
4. $£4\cdot50-93\frac{1}{2}p$
5. $\frac{1}{3}$ of 294
6. $19\frac{1}{2}p\times8$
7. $\frac{1}{6}$ of 720
8. $350\ g\times10$
9. $1\frac{1}{4}\ \ell\div5$
10. 0.96×7
11. $300-(7\times8)$
12. $£3\cdot24\div8$
13. $6.06+1.94$
14. $2\ m-75\ cm$
15. $5-1.86$
16. 7.5×7
17. $1\frac{1}{3}\times8$
18. $8.4\div6$
19. $14.04\div9$
20. $\frac{7}{8}$ of 96p

B
Write the answers only.

1.
$$\begin{array}{r}£\\0\cdot95\\13\cdot06\\15\cdot78\\+\ 1\cdot04\\\hline\end{array}$$

2.
$$\begin{array}{r}34.3\ m\\6.8\ m\\17.5\ m\\0.9\ m\\+\ 4.5\ m\\\hline\end{array}$$

3.
$$\begin{array}{rr}kg & g\\2 & 280\\ & 900\\1 & 450\\+2 & 650\\\hline\end{array}$$

4.
$$\begin{array}{r}3049\\-\ 876\\\hline\end{array}$$

5.
$$\begin{array}{r}20.370\ kg\\-\ 0.980\ kg\\\hline\end{array}$$

6.
$$\begin{array}{r}8.324\ m\\-6.657\ m\\\hline\end{array}$$

7.
$$\begin{array}{r}608\\\times9\\\hline\end{array}$$

8.
$$\begin{array}{r}£9\cdot75\\\times7\\\hline\end{array}$$

9.
$$\begin{array}{r}2\ m\ 30\ cm\\\times8\\\hline\end{array}$$

10. $8\overline{)8096}$
11. $6\overline{)£13\cdot20}$
12. $7\overline{)£4\cdot55}$

13. $3\overline{)7\ kg\ 500\ g}$
14. $5\overline{)16.25\ \ell}$
15. $9\overline{)8.280\ m}$

16. $\dfrac{88.5\ m}{5}$
17. $\dfrac{300\ kg}{8}$
18. $\dfrac{234\ mm}{9}$

C
Find how much the first quantity is greater than ($+$) or less than ($-$) the second.

1. 5.7 cm   81 mm
2. 154 cm   2.3 m
3. 6 m   3076 mm
4. 1437 m $1\frac{1}{4}$ km
5. $10\frac{1}{2}$ kg   7.750 kg
6. 1270 g   0.980 kg
7. $5\ \ell\ 700\ m\ell$ $8.1\ \ell$

D
Find by the shortest method.

1. $(17+17+17+17)+(23+23+23+23)$
2. $(12\times4)+(16\times4)+(20\times4)$
3. $80-16-16-16-16-16$
4. $150-(25+25+25+25+25)$
5. $(19\times2)+(3\times19)+(19\times4)$
6. $(7\times8)+(7\times8)+(7\times8)+(7\times8)+(7\times8)$
7. $(347\times7)-(347\times5)$
8. $(\frac{1}{2}$ of $392)+(\frac{1}{4}$ of $392)+(\frac{1}{8}$ of $392)$
9. $(\frac{3}{5}$ of $370)+(\frac{3}{10}$ of $370)$
10. $(\frac{5}{12}$ of $228)+(\frac{7}{12}$ of $228)$

E
1. Write the members of these sets.
Omit 1 and the number itself. The number of members in each set is given.

$T=\{$factors of $12\}$ 4 members
$Z=\{$factors of $20\}$ 4 members
$X=\{$factors of $24\}$ 6 members
$Y=\{$factors of $30\}$ 6 members
$W=\{$factors of $60\}$ 10 members

Find the missing factor from the set of factors of each of the numbers listed in the table.

	number	factors
2	39	1, 3, □, 39
3	91	1, 7, □, 91
4	85	1, 5, □, 85
5	133	1, 7, □, 133
6	161	1, 7, □, 161

F
Find the cost of each of the following. Work to the nearest penny.

1. 0.1 kg at £1·76 per kg
2. 10 cm at £5·32 per m
3. 100 mℓ at £1·27 per litre
4. 1.5 kg at 89p per $\frac{1}{2}$ kg
5. 750 g at £1·24 per kg
6. 20 ℓ at 85p per 5 litres
7. 45 ℓ at 94p per 5 litres

Triangles

A Triangles are named according to a their sides b their angles.

Look at the chart. It will remind you of important facts you have discovered.

Equilateral triangle	Isosceles triangle	Scalene triangle
3 equal sides 3 equal angles 3 lines of symmetry	2 equal sides opposite 2 equal angles 1 line of symmetry	sides and angles of different sizes no lines of symmetry

Acute-angled triangle — each angle is acute (less than 90°)

Obtuse-angled triangle — one angle is obtuse (more than 90°)

Right-angled triangle — one angle is 90°

The sum of the three angles of a triangle is 180°.

1 Use a ruler and set square to find which of the triangles below belong to each of the following sets.

E = {equilateral triangles} I = {isosceles triangles}

S = {scalene triangles} R = {right-angled triangles}

O = {obtuse-angled triangles} A = {acute-angled triangles}

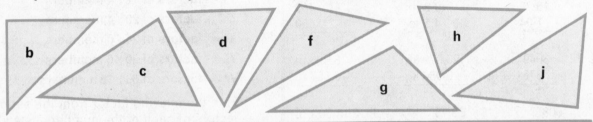

B

1 On stiff paper, draw and cut out a triangle with sides 30 mm 40 mm 50 mm.

2 Fit your triangle exactly over triangle **v**. You may twist your triangle or turn it over.

3 Find out whether:

a the angles of both triangles are the same size

b the sides of both triangles are the same length.

4 Are the two triangles the same shape and size exactly?

Remember
Shapes which are exactly the same shape and size are said to be **congruent**.

5 On stiff paper, draw and cut out these triangles.

triangle	lengths of sides
w	50 mm, 35 mm, 25 mm
x	30 mm, 30 mm, 30 mm
y	30 mm, 20 mm, 30 mm
z	35 mm, 25 mm, 43 mm

6 Take triangle **w** and find, by fitting, which of the triangles in Section **A** is congruent with it.

7 In the same way, find which triangle in Section **A** is congruent with:
triangle **x** triangle **y** triangle **z**.

Name each of the triangles **w, x, y** and **z**:

8 by its sides 9 by its angles.

Triangles   rigid and non-rigid shapes

A

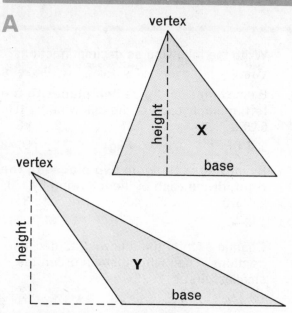

vertex

height

X

base

vertex

height

Y

base

1   Measure in mm the base of
triangle **X**   triangle **Y**.

> The height of a triangle is the length
> of a perpendicular drawn from the
> vertex to the base.

2   Measure the height of each triangle.

3   Measure in mm the sides of:
triangle **X**   triangle **Y**.

4   a   Draw each triangle **X** and **Y** in a
different position, so that the longest
side becomes the base.
   b   Draw and measure the height of each
triangle.

5   a   Draw each triangle again so that the
shortest side becomes the base.
   b   Draw and measure the height of each
triangle.

B

Obtain some plastic or cardboard strips
of different lengths and some fasteners.

1   Fit them together to
make several triangles
of different shapes.

2   Push each triangle
at the corners.
Does its shape alter?

> The triangle is a **rigid** (fixed) shape
> because its shape can only be altered
> by changing the length of its sides.

3   Use the strips to make a quadrilateral,
a pentagon and a hexagon.

quadrilateral
(4 sides)

pentagon
(5 sides)

hexagon
(6 sides)

4   Push each of these shapes at the corners.
What happens to the shape in each case?

5   Are the quadrilateral, the pentagon and
the hexagon rigid shapes?
Give the reason for your answer.

6   Take the quadrilateral again and fix a
cross-piece as shown below.

7   Try to alter its shape
by pushing at the
corners.
You discover that the
quadrilateral is now
a rigid shape.

8   How many triangles have you made in
the quadrilateral?

C

1   Copy this table.

number of sides in shape	3	4	5	6	7	8
number of cross-pieces	0					
number of triangles	1					

2   a   Complete it by finding how many cross-pieces and triangles must be used to make rigid
each of the shapes.   b   Find the simple rule which connects the numbers in each column.

3   How many   a   cross-pieces   b   triangles
are required to make rigid a shape   of 10 sides   of 12 sides?

Decimal fractions
tenths, hundredths, thousandths

A Write the following as decimals.

1 3 units 6 tenths 5 hundredths

2 4 tens 84 hundredths

3 709 hundredths

4 98 units 2 tenths

5 533 tenths

6 38 units 6 hundredths

Complete the following.

7 9.84 = ☐ units ☐ tenths ☐ hundredths
    = ☐ tenths ☐ hundredths

8 7.02 = ☐ tenths ☐ hundredths
    = ☐ hundredths

9 3.6 = ☐ tenths = ☐ hundredths

Write the value of each figure underlined.

10 <u>7</u>09.64   11 35 <u>0</u>19   12 90 3<u>5</u>7

13 2021.<u>7</u>3   14 £<u>5</u>0·38   15 £4<u>0</u>70·50

Write the following as decimal fractions.

16 $\frac{24}{100}$ 17 $\frac{30}{100}$ 18 $\frac{78}{100}$ 19 $\frac{59}{100}$

By moving each figure **two places to the left**, multiply each of the following by 100.

20 6.25   21 0.37   22 1.8

23 50.04 m   24 2.7 kg   25 £0·48

By moving each figure **two places to the right**, divide each of the following by 100.

26 293 570   27 405   28 34

29 £13·00   30 74 m   31 325 ℓ

Change each of the following to decimal fractions. Then write them in order, the smallest first.

32 $\frac{7}{10}$ $\frac{1}{2}$ $\frac{3}{4}$ $\frac{3}{5}$ 33 $\frac{7}{20}$ $\frac{9}{25}$ $\frac{3}{10}$ $\frac{36}{50}$

Change the following to vulgar fractions. Write each in its lowest terms.

34 0.8   35 0.05   36 0.25   37 0.88

B In the table, the 1 in the hundredths column is moved **one place to the right**. Its value, therefore, is 10 times smaller than one hundredth.

Th	H	T	U	t	h	
1	1	1	1 ·	1	1	1

decreases 10 times for each place

You must now find the value of **one tenth of one hundredth** or $\frac{1}{10}$ of $\frac{1}{100}$ or $\frac{1}{10}$ of $\frac{1}{10}$ of $\frac{1}{10}$ which will give the **third place of decimals**.

Look at the diagrams.

1 How many blocks like that marked **X** are there in the whole one?

2 How many blocks like that marked **Y** are there in:
   a block **X**   b the whole one?

3 How many blocks like that marked **Z** are there in:
   a block **Y**   b block **X**?

4 Without counting, how many blocks like the block marked **Z** are there in the **whole one**?

5 What fraction of the **whole one** is block **Z**?

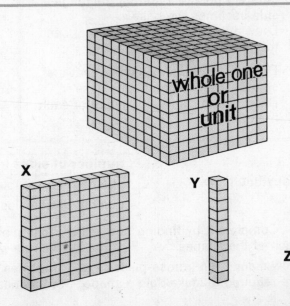

Decimal fractions
tenths, hundredths, thousandths

Refer to Section **B** on the opposite page.
Make sure you understand the following.

U	t	h	th
0 . 1			
0 . 0	1		
0 . 0	0	1	

Block **X** is $\frac{1}{10}$ of the whole one————————————————or→ 0 . 1

Block **Y** is $\frac{1}{10}$ of $\frac{1}{10}$ = $\frac{1}{100}$ of the whole one——or→ 0 . 0 1

Block **Z** is $\frac{1}{10}$ of $\frac{1}{10}$ of $\frac{1}{10}$ = $\frac{1}{1000}$ of the whole one——or→ 0 . 0 0 1

Remember   The figure in the **first place** after the decimal point is **tenths**.
The figure in the **second place** after the decimal point is **hundredths**.
The figure in the **third place** after the decimal point is **thousandths**.

A

1 Write in full each of the numbers in the table. The answer to the first example is:

a=3 units 2 hundredths 5 thousandths.

	H	T	U	t	h	th
a			3 .	0	2	5
b			7 .	3	0	7
c		4	0 .	8	4	1
d	5	0	6 .	9		
e			0 .	2	0	4

Draw a table and write these numbers:

2 105 tenths   3 261 tenths
4 44 hundredths   5 82 hundredths
6 1005 hundredths   7 1403 hundredths
8 125 thousandths   9 4254 thousandths
10 67 tenths 89 thousandths
11 $3\frac{59}{100}$ 12 $\frac{4187}{10}$ 13 $\frac{7002}{1000}$
14 eighty point nought nought four.

Write as decimals.

15 19 thousandths   16 503 hundredths
17 470 tenths   18 807 thousandths
19 5 thousandths   20 100 thousandths
21 3 tenths 8 thousandths
22 5004 thousandths
23 25 units 8 hundredths
24 10 units 4 thousandths

B

How many tenths in:
1 5.8   2 17.6   3 63?

How many hundredths in:
4 2.07   5 0.94   6 12.5?

How many thousandths in:
7 0.034   8 0.8   9 0.76
10 2.637   11 1.09   12 6.4?

Complete the following.
13 0.057 = ☐ hundredths ☐ thousandths
            = ☐ thousandths
14 6.004 = ☐ units ☐ thousandths
            = ☐ thousandths

Example   12.35 = $10+2+\frac{3}{10}+\frac{5}{100}$

In the same way, write each of the following.
15 20.026   16 3.805   17 0.327

Write as decimals.
18 $90+\frac{2}{10}+\frac{3}{100}$ 19 $5+\frac{4}{100}+\frac{9}{1000}$
20 $1+\frac{1}{10}+\frac{8}{100}$ 21 $30+\frac{1}{10}+\frac{4}{1000}$
22 $1-\frac{1}{1000}$ 23 $1-\frac{15}{100}$
24 $1-\frac{5}{1000}$ 25 $1-\frac{37}{100}$
26 $1-\frac{50}{1000}$ 27 $1-\frac{500}{1000}$

What is the value of each figure underlined in these numbers?
28 0.8<u>3</u>7   29 <u>5</u>04.07   30 6.0<u>7</u>3
31 29.<u>5</u>02   32 3.0<u>9</u>1   33 8.0<u>4</u>2

Decimal fractions
tenths, hundredths, thousandths

A Study this table. It shows many facts about the **decimal number system.**

Th	H	T	U	t	h	th
1000	100	10	1	0.1 $\frac{1}{10}$	0.01 $\frac{1}{100}$	0.001 $\frac{1}{1000}$
100×10 $10 \times 10 \times 10$ 10^3	10×10 10^2	10×1 10^1	1	$\frac{1}{10}$	$\frac{1}{10} \times \frac{1}{10}$	$\frac{1}{10} \times \frac{1}{10} \times \frac{1}{10}$

Remember the rules for **multiplying**:

by 10 Figures move **one place** to the **left**.
by 100 Figures move **two places** to the **left**.
by 1000. Figures move **three places** to the **left**.

H	T	U	t	h	th
	1	2.	7	4	
3	5	0.	6		
8	0	5.			

$10 \times$ —
$100 \times$ —
$1000 \times$ —

U	t	h	th
1.	2	7	4
3.	5	0	6
0.	8	0	5

Write the answers only.

1 50.4×10 2 0.076×10 3 83.52×10 4 3.002×10 5 1.369×100
6 10.101×100 7 15.5×100 8 0.24×1000 9 0.357×1000 10 0.086×1000

Remember the rules for **dividing**:

by 10 Figures move **one place** to the **right**.
by 100 Figures move **two places** to the **right**.
by 1000. Figures move **three places** to the **right**.

H	T	U	t
2	6	0.	5
3	0	9.	8
7	4	2.	

$\div 10$ →
$\div 100$ →
$\div 1000$ →

H	T	U	t	h	th
2	6.	0	5		
	3.	0	9	8	
	0.	7	4	2	

Write the answers only.

11 $508 \div 10$ 12 $3.27 \div 10$ 13 $0.46 \div 10$ 14 $91 \div 100$ 15 $6.2 \div 100$
16 $670 \div 100$ 17 $470 \div 1000$ 18 $1832 \div 1000$ 19 $75 \div 1000$ 20 $1001 \div 1000$

B

1
X	Y
480.4	

By how many times is the 4 marked **X** greater or less than the 4 marked **Y**?

2
X	Y
5.125	

By how many times is the 5 marked **Y** greater or less than the 5 marked **X**?

3 Find the difference between 70.0 and 19 thousandths.

Write the numbers in **4**, **5** and **6** in columns and find the total of each.

4 107 hundredths, 72 tenths, 4 tens
5 93 units, 18 tenths, 207 thousandths
6 13 hundreds, 90 units, 55 thousandths
7 Write the three answers in order of size, putting the smallest first.

C Write the answers only.

1 5.4×2 5 $9(0.809)$ 9 $4(1.75)$ 13 $14.4 \div 3$ 17 $4\overline{)9.0}$ 21 $6\overline{)0.816}$
2 4.05×3 6 $5(0.041)$ 10 $8(3.76)$ 14 $30.6 \div 5$ 18 $8\overline{)5.8}$ 22 $7\overline{)1.799}$
3 0.37×4 7 $6(0.076)$ 11 $5(7.8)$ 15 $1.26 \div 7$ 19 $5\overline{)6.2}$ 23 $9\overline{)9.081}$
4 3.25×8 8 $7(0.051)$ 12 $2(1.95)$ 16 $7.25 \div 2$ 20 $2\overline{)0.1}$ 24 $3\overline{)10.11}$

Decimal fractions   SI units

The units of measurement about which you have learned are SI units, or units based on SI units. SI is a symbol which stands for the International System of Units.

When using SI units, it is important that the symbols are written correctly, and it should be noted that a full stop is never used after a symbol unless the symbol is at the end of a sentence.

For example: millimetres mm

Study the chart which shows some of the correct symbols.

Notice that most of the units in general use are based on **thousands** and **thousandths**.

thousands	unit	thousandths
kilometre km	metre m	millimetre mm
kilogram kg	gram g	milligram mg
kilolitre kℓ	litre ℓ	millilitre mℓ

1 litre or 1 cubic decimetre = 1000 cm³

10 mm = 1 cm   100 cm = 1 m

A

Write as kilograms kg

1 1850 g   2   3420 g   3   2700 g

4 4090 g   5   600 g   6   352 g

Write as metres m

7 2836 mm   8   5350 mm   9   5900 mm

10 1009 mm   11   970 mm   12   400 mm

Write as kilometres km

13 3000 m   14   5500 m   15   650 m

16 4090 m   17   250 m   18   960 m

Write as litres ℓ

19 2200 mℓ   20   1280 mℓ   21   350 mℓ

22 800 mℓ   23   668 mℓ   24   725 mℓ

Write as grams g

25 1.274 kg   26   2.450 kg   27   1.070 kg

28 1.5 kg   29   2.75 kg   30   0.4 kg

Write as millimetres mm

31 3.175 m   32   1.380 m   33   0.166 m

34 2.5 m   35   0.9 m   36   3.25 m

Write as metres m

37 2.75 km   38   0.1 km   39   4.125 km

40 0.025 km   41   3.7 km   42   0.8 km

Write as millilitres mℓ

43 1.6 ℓ   44   3.25 ℓ   45   0.732 ℓ

46 0.85 ℓ   47   1.1 ℓ   48   4.3 ℓ

B

A sheet of paper is 0.1 mm thick. What would be the thickness of 1000 sheets:

1 in mm   2   in m?

How many lengths each measuring 35 mm can be cut from:

3 $3\frac{1}{2}$ m   4   7 m   5   14 m?

From Peter's home to school is 857 m. He makes the journey there and back twice a day. How many km does he travel:

6 each day   7   in five days?

In mother's shopping basket there were:

5 tins, each with a mass of 327 g
4 packets, each with a mass of 500 g
1 parcel with a mass of 1.250 kg.

Find the total mass of the goods:

8 in g   9   in kg.

The following are distances run by athletes in the European Games.

10 1500 m   11   10 000 m   12   4 × 400 m relay

Write each distance in km.

Below are some interesting facts about the Alpine Tunnel under Mont Blanc.

13 Write and complete the table.

length of tunnel	11.6 km	=	☐m
height of tunnel	4.8 m	=	☐mm
width of road	7 m	=	☐mm

maximum permitted dimensions:			
height of vehicles	4.15 m	=	☐mm
width of vehicles	2.50 m	=	☐mm

14 Find, from an atlas, the situation tunnel and discover the reason is important.

Making sure

A Turn to pages 13 and 14. Work sections **A** to **E** on both pages as quickly as possible. Mark the answers and correct any mistakes.

B Round off each of these numbers:

to the nearest whole one

1 $11\frac{5}{8}$ 2 7.6   3 18.25   4 99.05

to the nearest ten

5 63   6 115   7 238   8 182

to the nearest 100

9 352   10 1050   11 1991   12 3247

to the nearest 1000.

13 8086   14 30 603   15 84 308   16 10 640

17 Father was 11 minutes early for his train which departed at 12.06 p.m.
At what time did he arrive at the station?

Buses leave a hospital at 6.30 p.m. and then every 18 min until 8.00 p.m.

18 Write, in 24-hour clock times, when each bus leaves the hospital.

Three angles of a quadrilateral measure 98°, 127° and 45°.

19 Find the size of the fourth angle.

Which of the four angles are:

20 acute angles   21 obtuse angles?

22 Find the difference in degrees between temperatures of 13°C and −4°C.

C Write these numbers, placing a decimal point in each, so that:

the value of the 8 is 8 hundredths

1 908   2 58   3 1985   4 81   5 1008

the value of the 3 is three thousandths.

6 453   7 93   8 673   9 3   10 30

Draw these triangles.

11 Triangle **Y**
base 45 mm   sides 94 mm   60 mm

12 Triangle **Z**
base 60 mm   sides 45 mm   68 mm

In each of the triangles listed in the table, the size of each of two angles is given.

triangle	angles		
P	25°	65°	
Q	35°		80°
R		70°	70°
S	60°	60°	
T	44°		92°

13 Find, by calculation, the number of degrees in the third angle in each triangle.

14 Name each triangle according to
a its sides   b its angles.

D The diagram shows approximate distances in kilometres by road between certain towns.

How far is the return journey from:

1 Glasgow to Edinburgh

2 Edinburgh to Leeds via Carlisle

3 Preston to Glasgow via Carlisle?

4 A motorist travelled from Glasgow to Leeds via Carlisle at an average speed of 80 km/h.
How long, to the nearest half-hour, did the journey take?

5 A truck from Leeds calls at Newcastle, Edinburgh and Carlisle. It then returns to Leeds.
The truck travels at an average speed of 50 km/h, and the driver rests for $8\frac{1}{2}$ hours.
Find the time taken, to the nearest half-hour, for the whole journey.

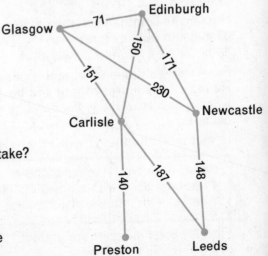

Money shopping

A

Find the change from 50p after spending:
1. 11p 2. $34\frac{1}{2}$p 3. 17p 4. 38p.

Find the change from £1 after spending:
5. 14p 6. 53p 7. $87\frac{1}{2}$p 8. 36p
9. 41p 10. 75p 11. 28p 12. $62\frac{1}{2}$p.

Find the change from £5 after spending:
13. £1·35 14. £3·82 15. £4·23 16. £1·$14\frac{1}{2}$.

Find the change from £10 after spending:
17. £3·59 18. £6·74 19. £2·09 20. £5·37
21. £1·18 22. £4·51 23. £7·02 24. £6·63.

Find the cost of:
25. 8 at $5\frac{1}{2}$p each 26. 6 at 19p each
27. 7 at 13p each 28. 5 at 98p each
29. 3 at £1·62 each 30. 4 at £1·75 each.

C

Find the cost of 10 if 1 costs:
1. 15p 2. $23\frac{1}{2}$p 3. £0·$14\frac{1}{2}$ 4. £0·97
5. £1·11 6. £2·50 7. £1·$25\frac{1}{2}$ 8. £3·72.

Find the cost of 1 if 10 cost:
9. 75p 10. £6·10 11. £3·45 12. £10·50
13. £15 14. £22·50 15. £18·20 16. £16·25.

Find the cost of 100 if 1 costs:
17. 3p 18. 16p 19. 38p 20. $9\frac{1}{2}$p
21. 10p 22. £0·15 23. £0·$72\frac{1}{2}$ 24. £0·$06\frac{1}{2}$.

Find the cost of 1 if 100 cost:
25. £1 26. £16 27. £23 28. £120
29. £136 30. £111 31. £3·50 32. £105·50.

B

Choose the best approximation for each of the following.

1	37p × 6	£2·80	£1·80	£2·40
2	$24\frac{1}{2}$p × 4	£1·00	£0·80	£1·20
3	96p × 9	£8·00	£9·00	£10·00
4	2.75 ℓ × 5	10 ℓ	15 ℓ	12 ℓ
5	£23·96 ÷ 4	£5	£4	£6
6	£39·20 ÷ 8	£4·00	£5·00	£6·00
7	£20·58 ÷ 3	£5·50	£6·50	£8·00
8	64.4 kg ÷ 7	8 kg	9 kg	10 kg

9. Find the difference between your approximation and the actual answer to each of the questions 1-8.

D

Find the missing amount or sum of money.

	given in payment	goods purchased	change
1	£1 note	1 at 54p	□p
2	3 FIFTIES	4 at 28p	□p
3	□	3 at 15p	5p
4	□	$1\frac{1}{2}$kg at 45p per kg	$32\frac{1}{2}$p
5	a FIFTY	□ at 12p	14p
6	£3	4 at □p	20p
7	a FIFTY	3 at $14\frac{1}{2}$p	□p
8	□	6 at 85p	90p
9	£2	□ at 5p	25p
10	a FIFTY	$1\frac{1}{4}$ ℓ at 32p per ℓ	□p

E

The following ingredients are required when making twenty Queen cakes.

100 g butter	100 g caster sugar
150 g self-raising flour	
2 eggs	25 mℓ of milk
100 g currants	pinch of salt

When the ingredients are mixed, the mixture is placed in equal quantities into twenty cake cases.

1. Using the prices given, find the total cost of the ingredients for the 20 cakes.

butter 65p $\frac{1}{2}$ kg   currants 55p per 500 g
eggs 10 for 55p   milk 5p for 250 mℓ
self-raising flour 30p per kg
caster sugar 75p per kg

Allow $22\frac{1}{2}$p extra for the twenty cake cases, the salt and for baking.

2. What is the cost of one cake?

Graphs

A The children in class 3 at Alton School had a test of 50 number facts every two weeks.

The children made graphs of their results. Some of them are given so that you can compare the progress of various children.

Look at Angela Smith's graph.

Angela Smith Number test record

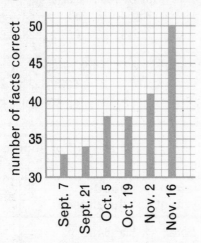

What information is given on:
1 the vertical axis 2 the horizontal axis?

Why is the scale on the vertical axis numbered:
3 from 30 and not from 0
4 from 30 to 50 and no further?

On which date was the test worked for:
5 the first time 6 the last time?

During which two weeks was there:
7 no improvement
8 the most improvement?

9 Write the number of facts she had correct on each date she took the test.

This table gives Andrew Biggs' results.

Sept. 7	Sept. 21	Oct. 5	Oct. 19	Nov. 2	Nov. 16
18	23	32	36	42	47

10 Draw a graph, like Angela's, to show his scores. You must alter the vertical scale.

During which period did Andrew make:
11 the most improvement 12 the least?

Look again at Angela's and Andrew's scores.

13 Whose average score do you think is the greater?

14 Work out their average scores and see if you chose correctly.

B Look at Peter Gray's graph.

Peter Gray Number test record

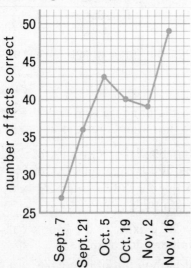

Peter marked each of his scores with a dot and then joined each of the dots with a thin line.

1 In what way is Peter's progress different from that of Angela or Andrew?

Find:
2 Peter's scores 3 his average score.

4 Compare his average score with Angela's and Andrew's. What do you discover?

5 Which of the three children made the most steady progress?
Look at the graphs and give a reason for your answer.

What do you notice about the slope of the line of the graph when the results:
6 improve rapidly 7 improve slowly
8 remain the same 9 get worse?

Graphs

A **Alan Day** Number test record

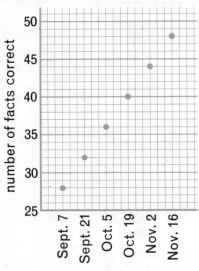

Alan Day made his record by marking each score with a dot, in the same way as Peter Gray.

1 Draw this table and complete it to show Alan's score for each test.

Sept. 7	Sept. 21	Oct. 5	Oct. 19	Nov. 2	Nov. 16

2 Find his average score.

3 By how many does Alan's score increase each time?

In what way is his record different from:

4 Angela's   5 Andrew's   6 Peter's?

7 Place your ruler across the points. What do you find?

B These are the records of Susan and Joan.

	Sept. 7	Sept. 21	Oct. 5	Oct. 19	Nov. 2	Nov. 16
Susan	14	20	26	32	38	44
Joan	25	28	31	34	37	40

1 Find Susan's average score.

2 Find Joan's average score to the nearest whole one.

For each test, by how many does:

3 Susan's score increase

4 Joan's score increase?

5 Plot Susan's scores and join the points. What kind of line have you drawn?

6 Plot Joan's scores and join the points. What kind of line have you drawn?

What you have discovered is important.

> When quantities **increase at the same rate**, the graph which is made will be a straight-line graph which rises.

7 What happens to the slope of the line if the quantities **decrease** at the same rate?

C

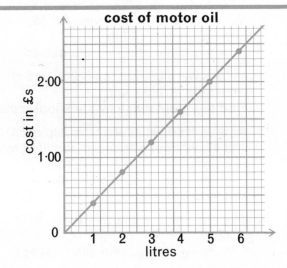

cost of motor oil

Straight-line graphs can be used as **ready reckoners**. This graph shows the cost of motor oil at 40p per litre.

From the graph, find the cost of:

1 2 litres   2 5 litres   3 $6\frac{1}{2}$ litres.

What quantity of oil can be bought for:

4 £1·20   5 £1·80   6 £2·20?

Copy the graph and extend it to show costs up to 15 litres. Find the cost of:

7 9 litres   8 12 litres   9 15 litres.

How many litres can be bought for:

10 £4·40   11 £5·20   12 £3·20?

Long multiplication

A

Multiply by 10	1 236	2 509	3 390
	4 7.4	5 24.6	6 3.28

To multiply a number by 20
First multiply the number by 10 and then multiply the answer by 2.

Multiply by 20	7 73	8 207	9 340
	10 26.8	11 1.96	12 0.83

Multiply by 30	13 87	14 90	15 163
	16 8.56	17 150.2	18 2.03

Write the answers only.

19 807×70 20 48×90 21 3.66×40

22 4.085×60 23 0.64×80 24 19.5×30

25 0.023×70 26 50×1.3 27 20×0.15

Write the answers only.

28 $£0.67 \times 30$ 29 $£0.09 \times 70$

30 $£2.48 \times 40$ 31 $£2.05 \times 50$

B

Look at the example below.

$$
\begin{array}{r}
57 \\
\times 38 \\
\hline
1710 \\
456 \\
\hline
2166 \\
\hline
\end{array}
\begin{array}{l}
= 57 \times 30 \\
= 57 \times\ 8 \\
= 57 \times 38
\end{array}
$$

Copy and complete.

1
$$
\begin{array}{r}
86 \\
\times 29 \\
\end{array}
$$
     $= 86 \times 20$
     $= 86 \times\ 9$
     $= 86 \times \overline{29}$

2
$$
\begin{array}{r}
67 \\
\times 48 \\
\end{array}
$$
     $= 67 \times 40$
     $= 67 \times\ 8$
     $= 67 \times \overline{48}$

In the same way, set down and work the following.

3 94	4 77	5 56	6 45
$\times 57$	$\times 28$	$\times 69$	$\times 32$

Find the product of:

7 34 and 26   8 75 and 18   9 25 and 24

10 81 and 45   11 76 and 37   12 92 and 63.

Find these answers in £s.

13 $38p \times 15$ 14 $19p \times 25$ 15 $52p \times 27$

16 $46p \times 19$ 17 $63p \times 53$ 18 $85p \times 64$

C

Look at the following example.

$$
\begin{array}{r}
£ \\
1\cdot86 \\
\times 29 \\
\hline
37\cdot20 \\
16\cdot74 \\
\hline
53\cdot94 \\
\hline
\end{array}
\begin{array}{l}
= £1\cdot86 \times 20 \\
= £1\cdot86 \times\ 9 \\
= £1\cdot86 \times 29
\end{array}
$$

Copy and complete.

1
$$
\begin{array}{r}
£ \\
0\cdot68 \\
\times 32 \\
\end{array}
$$
     $= £0\cdot68 \times 30$
     $= £0\cdot68 \times\ 2$
     $= £0\cdot68 \times \overline{32}$

2
$$
\begin{array}{r}
£ \\
2\cdot80 \\
\times 19 \\
\end{array}
$$
     $= £2\cdot80 \times 10$
     $= £2\cdot80 \times\ 9$
     $= £2\cdot80 \times \overline{19}$

Set down and work the following.

3 $£1\cdot78 \times 24$ 4 $£3\cdot28 \times 16$

5 $£4\cdot50 \times 26$ 6 $£0\cdot87 \times 21$

D

Find the value of:

1 16^2 2 35^2 3 15^3 4 18^3.

5 By how many is 55×37 greater than 55×19?

6 Find the product of 32 and 17.
Now write the answers only to each of the following.

7 3.20×17 8 $£0\cdot32 \times 17$ 9 32×1.7

10 $3.2 m \times 17$ 11 320×17 12 $17p \times 32$

13 Mother paid £1·75 per week for 15 weeks into a Christmas Club.
How much did she save altogether?

14 40 toys were bought for £22·80 and all were sold at 75p each.
Find the profit made by the shopkeeper.

15 At a concert, 93 adults paid 90p each, and 47 children were each admitted for half-price.
Find the total amount taken at the concert.

16 The gross mass of a tin of tomatoes is 426 g.
Find, in kg, the gross mass of 24 tins.

Long division

A

| **Divide by 10** | 1 600 | 2 890 | 3 770 |
| | 4 260 | 5 110 | 6 420 |

To divide a number by 20
First divide the number by 10 and then divide the answer by 2.

| **Divide by 20** | 7 240 | 8 420 | 9 560 |
| | 10 780 | 11 900 | 12 340 |

To divide a number by 30
First divide the number by 10 and then divide the answer by 3.

| **Divide by 30** | 13 420 | 14 360 | 15 570 |
| | 16 600 | 17 750 | 18 810 |

Write the answers only.

19 $320 \div 80$ 20 $270 \div 90$ 21 $540 \div 60$

22 $50)\overline{450}$ 23 $40)\overline{240}$ 24 $70)\overline{560}$

25 $80)\overline{640}$ 26 $70)\overline{630}$ 27 $90)\overline{810}$

B

Look at the following example in which there is a remainder.

> First divide the tens by the tens.
> (The tens are shown in **heavy type**.)
> How many **4**s in **29**? 7   7 rem. 16
> 7 is the 'trial' figure. $40)\overline{296}$
> Try 7. 40×7 ──────▶ 280
>   16 rem.

Copy and complete.

1
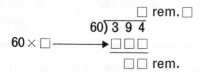

Set down and work the following.

2 $50)\overline{423}$ 3 $30)\overline{255}$ 4 $70)\overline{557}$

5 $90)\overline{581}$ 6 $80)\overline{439}$ 7 $60)\overline{352}$

8 Find the value of each letter.
$(50 \times 7) + r = 392$ $(20 \times 9) + s = 194$
$(60 \times 3) + t = 213$ $(70 \times 8) + u = 625$
$(90 \times v) + 7 = 637$ $(30 \times w) + 24 = 204$
$(50 \times x) + 45 = 295$ $(40 \times y) + 38 = 318$
$423p = z$ FIFTIES $+ 23$ pence

C

It is usually necessary when finding a 'trial' figure to round off the divisor to the nearest 10. Look at the example.

> First divide the tens by the tens.
> 42 rounded off is 40.
> How many **4**s in **26**? 6   6 rem. 9
> 6 is the 'trial' figure. $42)\overline{261}$
> Try 6. 42×6 ──────▶ 252
>   9 rem.

Copy and complete.
1 $52)\overline{419}$
52 rounded off is 50.
How many 5s in 41?   ☐ rem. ☐
☐ is the trial figure. $52)\overline{4\ 1\ 9}$
Try ☐. $52 \times$ ☐ ──────▶ ☐☐☐
                                  ☐ rem.

Work the following.

2 $41)\overline{340}$ 3 $33)\overline{232}$ 4 $22)\overline{179}$

5 $43)\overline{225}$ 6 $31)\overline{162}$ 7 $52)\overline{320}$

8 $73)\overline{299}$ 9 $62)\overline{500}$ 10 $51)\overline{468}$

D

Look at the example.

> 38 rounded off is 40.   6 rem. 13
> How many **4**s in **24**? $38)\overline{241}$
> Try 6. 38×6 ──────▶ 228
>   13 rem.

Copy and complete.
1 $29)\overline{210}$
29 rounded off is ☐.   ☐ rem. ☐
How many ☐s in 21? $29)\overline{2\ 1\ 0}$
Try ☐. $29 \times$ ☐ ──────▶ ☐☐☐
                                  ☐ rem.

Work the following.

2 $19)\overline{178}$ 3 $27)\overline{155}$ 4 $18)\overline{161}$

5 $49)\overline{423}$ 6 $37)\overline{251}$ 7 $49)\overline{468}$

8 $36)\overline{245}$ 9 $58)\overline{426}$ 10 $66)\overline{370}$

11 Write a reason for rounding off the divisors to the nearest 10.

Write the largest possible remainder when a whole number is divided by:

12 30   13 40   14 37   15 59.

Long division

A Sometimes the 'trial' figure gives a product which is too large or too small.
You may have to use a figure which is one more or one less than the trial figure.
Look at the examples.

44 rounded off is 40.
How many **4**s in **36**?

Try 9. $44 \times 9 = 396$ 8 rem. 9
The product 396 is too large. $44\overline{)361}$
Try 8. 44×8 ————→ 352
           9 rem.

25 rounded off is 30.
How many **3**s in **16**?

Try 5. $25 \times 5 = 125$ 6 rem. 13
The product 125 is too small. $25\overline{)163}$
Try 6. $25 \times 6 = 150$ ————→ 150
           13 rem.

Work the following.

1 $36\overline{)255}$	2 $27\overline{)244}$	3 $23\overline{)190}$
7 $22\overline{)161}$	8 $35\overline{)282}$	9 $31\overline{)180}$

4 $32\overline{)271}$	5 $26\overline{)184}$	6 $41\overline{)360}$
10 $28\overline{)170}$	11 $18\overline{)146}$	12 $44\overline{)364}$

B Look at the example.

Divide 99 tens by 22.   45 rem. 8
22 rounded off is 20. $22\overline{)998}$
Try 4 (tens). 22×4 tens ————→ 880
Divide 118 units by 22.   118
Try 5. 22×5 units ————→ 110
           8 rem.

Work the following.

1 $29\overline{)730}$	6 $53\overline{)860}$	11 $24\overline{)590}$
2 $31\overline{)570}$	7 $27\overline{)661}$	12 $61\overline{)990}$
3 $36\overline{)692}$	8 $35\overline{)820}$	13 $28\overline{)500}$
4 $21\overline{)910}$	9 $79\overline{)959}$	14 $33\overline{)781}$
5 $46\overline{)800}$	10 $18\overline{)673}$	15 $58\overline{)837}$

C Look at the example.

Divide 177 tens by 49.   36 rem. 6
49 rounded off is 50. $49\overline{)1770}$
Try 3 (tens). 49×3 tens ————→ 1470
Divide 300 units by 49.   300
Try 6. 49×6 ————→ 294
           6 rem.

Work the following.

1 $43\overline{)1161}$	6 $21\overline{)1570}$	11 $63\overline{)1403}$
2 $49\overline{)1764}$	7 $57\overline{)1600}$	12 $55\overline{)1772}$
3 $29\overline{)1079}$	8 $72\overline{)2460}$	13 $16\overline{)1286}$
4 $51\overline{)2601}$	9 $33\overline{)1421}$	14 $25\overline{)2332}$
5 $38\overline{)1776}$	10 $19\overline{)1250}$	15 $67\overline{)1991}$

D Work the following.
Think carefully where to put the decimal point in each answer.

1 $15\overline{)£6·45}$	7 $24\overline{)£12·48}$
2 $18\overline{)£11·52}$	8 $19\overline{)£14·06}$
3 $21\overline{)£18·06}$	9 $17\overline{)£21·25}$
4 $29\overline{)£7·25}$	10 $16\overline{)£39·36}$
5 $31\overline{)£17·05}$	11 $14\overline{)£42·84}$
6 $23\overline{)£3·68}$	12 $23\overline{)£63·25}$

When working long division examples, first find an approximate answer.

Example $489 \div 52$
Approximation $500 \div 50 = 10$

Find approximate answers to the following.

13 $359 \div 39$	16 $618 \div 22$
14 $1337 \div 98$	17 $909 \div 29$
15 $£44·16 \div 15$	18 $£73·50 \div 24$

19 Now find the actual answers.
Compare them with your approximations.

Long multiplication and division

A

Find an approximation to each of the following from the numbers in the boxes.

1. 21×62
2. 192×49
3. 28×73
4. 46×85
5. 4.25×3.1
6. 9.85×61

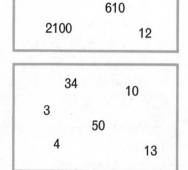

10 000		4500
1200		
	610	
2100		12

7. $1485 \div 32$
8. $150.96 \div 14.9$
9. $678 \div 19$
10. $1305 \div 96$
11. $2.099 \div 0.51$
12. $18.55 \div 5.7$

	34	10
3		
	50	
4		13

By rounding off each of the numbers to the nearest 10, find approximate answers to the following.

13. 39×21 14. 83×48 15. 57×19
16. $452 \div 28$ 17. $1736 \div 18$ 18. $1056 \div 23$

Now find the correct answers to questions **13** to **18**.

19. Fifteen times a number is one thousand and twenty. Find the number.

In each of the following examples some of the figures have been missed out.

Write and complete each example.

20.
```
    □□
  × 3 9
  ─────
  □□□□
   □□□
  ─────
  2 1 8 4
```

21.
```
    4 3
  × 7 □
  ─────
  □□□□
   3 8 7
  ─────
  □□□□
```

22.
```
      37
  □□)703
```

23.
```
         7 5 rem. 1
  29)□□□□
```

24. How many times can 32 be subtracted from 1888?

25. Find the value of each letter.

$19 \times c = 1083$

$57 = \dfrac{1311}{d}$

$\dfrac{£4.72}{16} = e$

$9f + 15f = 432$

26. What is the total of 24 added 63 times?

B

A farmer had 480 eggs to pack into boxes. How many boxes would he require if each box held:

1. 15 eggs
2. 16 eggs
3. 20 eggs
4. 24 eggs?

5. How many boxes would be filled if each box held 18 eggs?

6. How many eggs would be left over?

7. 25 ice-cream bricks were bought for £3·75. They were sold at 19p each. How much profit was made altogether?

8. How much will 25 family packets of crisps cost at 28p per packet?

9. 36 litres of orangeade cost £11·52. Find the cost of 1 litre.

10. A car travels 14 km per litre of petrol. How much petrol, to the nearest litre, is used for a journey of 315 km?

11. If a car uses 46 litres of petrol to travel 736 km, how many km per litre is that?

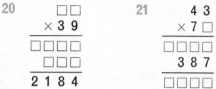

Portable TV

£247 cash

or

24 monthly payments of £12·50

12. How much is saved by paying cash for the portable TV set?

13. Mr. Jones will pay £3760 for his new car. This amount is divided into 40 equal payments. How much is each payment?

14.  £0·56 × 37   Timothy worked this example on his calculator. The answer given was £207·2 which was wrong. Find the correct answer and then give a reason for his error when using his calculator.

15. How much greater in length is 73 mm × 54   than   73 mm × 30?

Puzzle corner

A Find the missing numbers in each of the following series.

1 ☐, ☐, ☐, 7, 11, 16, 22
2 2, 4, 3, 9, 4, ☐, ☐, ☐
3 ☐, ☐, 8, 16, 32, 64
4 1, 4, 9, 16, 25, ☐, ☐, ☐
5 2.4, 1.2, 0.6, ☐, ☐
6 10, 5, 2½, ☐, ☐

7 In the example there are two additions. Fill in the missing digits, using them once only, so that the total is 100.

```
      ☐☐
      1 5
  + ☐☐
      ☐☐
  +   2
    1 0 0
```

8 The average age of three children is 9 years 8 months.
Tony's age is 9 years 1 month.
Ann's age is 9 years 11 months.
How old is Carol?

B

1 Arrange the numbers in the diagram in order, the smallest first.

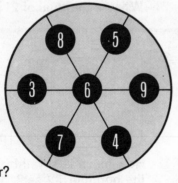

2 In the order of the numbers, which is the middle number?

Find the diameter on which the numbers 3, 6 and 9 are shown.
3 What is the total of the three numbers?

4 Check the total of the numbers on each of the other diameters. What do you find?

5 Make a similar diagram using this set of numbers.
{10, 11, 12, 13, 14, 15, 16}
Think carefully which member is placed in the centre of the circle.

Make sure the total of the three numbers on each diameter is the same.

C

1 Write all the odd numbers greater than a thousand you can make by re-arranging the digits **9, 1, 6, 5**.

In the following examples, write the sign +, −, ×, ÷ or = in place of ●.
2 (4 ● 3) ● (20 ● 8)
3 (7 ● 6) ● (9 ● 4)
4 7 ● 56 ● 8
5 (45 ● 9) ● (100 ● 20)
6 8½ ● 17 ● 8½

Write the answers only to the following.
7 1111−1010
8 (250+250)×10
9 (479×99)+479
10 (2×187)−(187+187)
11 (593×3×2)÷6
12 (10p×20)−3 FIFTIES

D Copy these number patterns.

The sum of the dots in each pattern is called a **triangular number**.
1 Find the first three triangular numbers shown above and then find and draw the next three triangular numbers.
2 Ann has enough money to spend 30p each day for 20 days.
How long will her money last if she spends 25p each day?
3 Tim saved £12 in 40 weeks.
How long did it take him to save £7·50 at the same rate?
4 Clare can swim 3 times as far as Peter, but only half as far as Jane who can swim 450 metres. How far can each swim?
5 What number, when multiplied by 9, is increased by 80?

Circles radius and diameter

A

1 Draw a circle of the same size as the diagram.

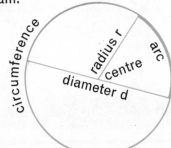

2 Name and write in mm the length of the measurement you used to set the compasses.

Draw a circle with a radius:

3 twice as long as the given circle

4 half as long as the given circle.

5 In each circle, draw several radii.

6 By measuring, show that all radii of the same circle are equal in length.

7 Draw three more circles of different sizes.

8 In each circle, draw several diameters.

9 At which point in the circle do they intersect (cut each other)?

10 By measuring, show that all the **diameters** in the same circle are equal in length.

11 Compare the length of the radius with the length of the diameter in each circle.

You should have found:

$$d = 2 \times r \quad \text{or} \quad d = 2r \qquad r = \frac{d}{2}$$
when d is the number of units in the diameter and r the number of units in the radius.

Find the diameter of a circle if the radius is:

12 3.7 cm   13 59 mm   14 2.75 m.

Find the radius of a circle if the diameter is:

15 74 mm   16 2.5 m   17 3.58 m.

Look again at the diagram in question **1**. Write sentences which describe in any circle:

18 a radius   19 a diameter

20 the circumference 21 an arc.

Carefully compare with the answer book what you have written

B

1 Measure the diameter in mm and draw the circle.

2 Use a set square to draw two diameters which are perpendicular to each other.

3 How many angles are there at the centre of the circle?

4 How many degrees are there in each?

5 How many degrees are there at the centre of the circle?

6 What shape can you make by joining the ends of the diameters?

In the circle shade:

7 a semicircle, red   8 a quadrant, blue.

9 Draw a semicircle with a diameter of 84 mm.

10 Mark any point on its circumference and join it to each end of the diameter.

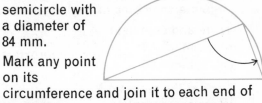

11 Use a set square to measure the angle at the circumference.

12 What is the name of this angle?

13 Mark three other points on the circumference and repeat the exercise.

14 Draw several semicircles of different sizes and repeat the exercise again.

15 Write what you have discovered about the angle at the circumference of any semicircle.

Circles   radius, diameter, circumference

A

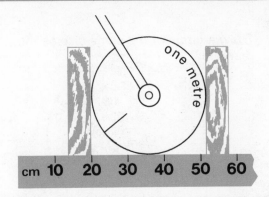

1. Get a metre trundle wheel and write its circumference in cm.
2. Using a metre rule as shown, find to the nearest cm the diameter of the wheel.
3. How many times approximately is the circumference greater than the diameter?
4. Write and complete:
$$\frac{\text{circumference}}{\text{diameter}} \quad \text{or} \quad \frac{c}{d} = \frac{\square\text{cm}}{\square\text{cm}}.$$

B

Diagrams **X** and **Y** below show circular objects of given diameters.

Each circular object is rolled along a metre rule for one revolution.

Two marks show the length of each circumference.

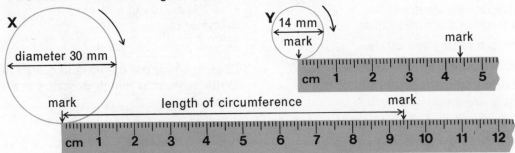

In diagram **X**, what is the measurement in mm of:
1. the circumference 2 the diameter?
3. How many times, approximately, is the circumference greater than the diameter?
4. Write and complete:
$$\frac{c}{d} = \frac{\square\text{mm}}{\square\text{mm}} \qquad \frac{c}{d} \text{ is } \square \text{ times approximately.}$$

Look at the diagram **Y**.
5. Write and complete:
$$\frac{c}{d} = \frac{\square\text{mm}}{\square\text{mm}} \qquad \frac{c}{d} \text{ is } \square \text{ times approximately.}$$

On a piece of thin card, draw and cut out these circles.
6. circle M, radius 21 mm
7. circle N, radius 28 mm

Measure in mm the circumference of:
8. circle M   9   circle N.
10. Find, in each case, approximately how many times the circumference is greater than the diameter by completing the following.
$$\frac{c}{d} = \frac{\square\text{mm}}{\square\text{mm}} \qquad \frac{c}{d} \text{ is } \square \text{ times approximately.}$$

C

Get a penny.

Measure in mm:
1. the diameter
2. the circumference.
3. Find the approximate relationship or ratio of the circumference to the diameter.

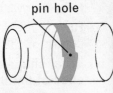

4. Get a jam jar and measure its diameter.
5. Then measure its circumference by using a paper strip.
6. Find the approximate ratio of the circumference to the diameter.

Circles radius, diameter, circumference

A

The drawing shows how Robert measured the circumference of a circular plastic bottle.

He wound a piece of string round the bottle exactly 10 times.

He then measured the string.

Its length was 188 cm.

1 How many circumferences has he measured?

Find the circumference of the bottle
2 in cm   3 in mm.

4 Write a reason why a more accurate measurement is obtained by winding the string round the bottle several times instead of once.

5 Why did Robert choose to wind the string round the bottle 10 times?

6 Estimate, in mm, the diameter of the bottle.

B Collect several circular objects, e.g. bottles, jars, lids, plates, wheels.

Use a suitable method to measure the circumference and the diameter of each in mm, or to the nearest cm.

Draw the table and enter the results.

Include those from page 56 sections **B** and **C**.

circular object	c	d	$\frac{c}{d}$	approx. value $\frac{c}{d}$
circle **X**	94 mm	30 mm	$\frac{94}{30}$	
circle **Y**		14 mm		
penny				

If you have worked carefully, you will have discovered that the length of the circumference of a circle is a little more than 3 times the length of the diameter.

The ratio $\dfrac{\text{circumference}}{\text{diameter}}$ is called by the Greek letter π (pi).

The approximate value of π is 3.14 or $3\frac{1}{7}$.

$c = \pi \times d$ or πd $c = \pi \times 2 \times r$ or $2\pi r$ when **c, d** and **r** are numbers of length units.

C Using $\pi = 3.14$, find the length of the circumference of each of the following circles if the radius is:

1 10 cm   2 20 mm   3 1 m   4 25 cm.

Using $\pi = 3\frac{1}{7}$, find the length of the circumference of each of the following circles if the diameter is:

5 14 cm   6 70 mm   7 42 cm   8 0.98 m.

Use $\pi = 3.14$ in working the following.

9 The diameter of a car wheel is 60 cm. Find to the nearest cm how far the car travels for one turn of the wheel.

10 Now write the answer to the nearest $\frac{1}{2}$ m.

11 Approximately how far, in metres, does the car travel for 100 turns of the wheel?

Two boys worked together in the playground to mark out a circle of 2 m diameter, using a piece of string and a piece of chalk.

12 What was the length of the string?

13 Describe what they did to mark out the circle.

14 Find the circumference of the circle to the nearest metre.

15 If the boys then drew another circle of twice the radius, what would be its circumference to the nearest metre?

16 Use a metre trundle wheel to measure the circumference of circles and semicircles marked out on games pitches in the playground and on the playing-field.

Percentages

A The drawing shows an area paved with square slabs of three different colours.

1 How many slabs were used to cover the area?

Count the number of slabs of each colour.

Then write and complete:

2 ☐ slabs out of 100 are coloured ▨

3 ☐ slabs out of 100 are coloured ☐

4 ☐ slabs out of 100 are coloured ▨.

5 What fraction of the 100 slabs is in each of the colours?

6 Write each of the answers as a decimal fraction.

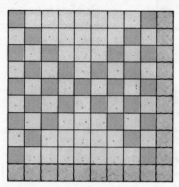

B Mary worked three number tests, each of 100 items. The table gives her scores.

	test A	test B	test C
score	63	72	78

Complete the following.

1 In test A, she scored ☐ out of 100.

2 In test B, she scored ☐ out of 100.

3 In test C, she scored ☐ out of 100.

Write each of Mary's results:

4 as a fraction

5 as a decimal fraction.

In each of the same tests, John scored 43, 51 and 59.
Write each of his results:

6 as 'so many' out of 100

7 as a fraction   8 as a decimal fraction.

C

> A short way of writing **'out of 100'** is **'per cent'** or by the sign **%**.
> **23 out of 100** or $\frac{23}{100}$ or **0.23** can be written as **23%**.

Write each of the following as a percentage using the sign %.

1 29 out of 100   2 $\frac{53}{100}$ 3 0.88

4 37 out of 100   5 $\frac{4}{100}$ 6 0.46

7 62 out of 100   8 $\frac{100}{100}$ 9 0.05

Write each of these percentages as a decimal fraction and then as a fraction in its lowest terms.

10 50%   11 20%   12 10%   13 15%

14 77%   15 25%   16 84%   17 9%

D In the diagrams below, one small square is $\frac{1}{100}$ or 0.01 of each whole one.

X   Y   Z

In which diagram is this amount shaded?

1 $\frac{1}{2}$ or $\frac{5}{10}$ 2 $\frac{1}{10}$ 3 $\frac{1}{4}$

Write and complete the following.

4 $\frac{1}{10}$ = 0.1 = ☐ out of 100 = ☐%

5 $\frac{9}{10}$ = ☐ = ☐ out of 100 = ☐%

6 $\frac{3}{10}$ = ☐ = ☐ out of 100 = ☐%

7 $\frac{7}{10}$ = ☐ = ☐ out of 100 = ☐%

8 $\frac{5}{10}$ or $\frac{1}{2}$ = ☐ = ☐ out of 100 = ☐%

9 $\frac{1}{4}$ = ☐ = ☐ out of 100 = ☐%

10 $\frac{3}{4}$ = ☐ = ☐ out of 100 = ☐%

> Vulgar fractions, decimal fractions and percentages express the same fraction in different ways.

Percentages

A

1 Draw and complete this table.

vulgar fraction	$\frac{1}{2}$	$\frac{1}{4}$	$\frac{3}{4}$	$\frac{1}{5}$ or $\frac{2}{10}$	$\frac{2}{5}$ or $\frac{4}{10}$	$\frac{3}{5}$ or $\frac{6}{10}$	$\frac{4}{5}$ or $\frac{8}{10}$	$\frac{1}{10}$			
decimal fraction									0.3		0.9
percentage										70%	

Check your answers and then study and learn all the facts. Ask your partner to test you.

B

Find the value of:

1 50% of 250

2 25% of 96

3 10% of 1000

4 75% of 120

5 50% of £8·00

6 25% of £0·80

7 10% of £1·50

8 75% of £1·60

9 50% of £3·74

10 10% of £5·20.

Find the value of:

	11 10%	12 30%	13 70%	of	**160**
	14 10%	15 30%	16 80%	of	**£2·40**
	17 10%	18 40%	19 60%	of	**5.800 m**
	20 10%	21 70%	22 90%	of	**3.700 kg**
	23 10%	24 80%	25 100%	of	**4.200 ℓ.**

C

Jean and Peter made a count of a all the motor vehicles b all the private cars which passed the school during certain periods of the day. The numbers are given below.

period of time	09.00 – 09.15	10.00 – 10.15	11.00 – 11.15	12.00 – 12.15
private cars	81	39	18	17
total of vehicles	100	50	25	20

Because the total number of vehicles was different in each case, it was not clear from the table during which period the highest proportion of the total was private cars.

Jean and Peter decided to find the percentage for each period.

Look at the count they made and then write and complete questions **1** to **4**.

09.00 – 09.15
1 81 out of 100 $= \frac{\square}{100} = \square\%$

10.00 – 10.15
2 39 out of 50 $= \frac{\square}{50} = \frac{\square}{100} = \square\%$

11.00 – 11.15
3 18 out of 25 $= \frac{\square}{25} = \frac{\square}{100} = \square\%$

12.00 – 12.15
4 17 out of 20 $= \frac{\square}{20} = \frac{\square}{100} = \square\%$

D

Write each of the following
a as a fraction with a denominator of 100
b as a percentage.

1 $\frac{9}{20}$ 2 $\frac{8}{25}$ 3 $\frac{47}{50}$ 4 $\frac{13}{20}$ 5 $\frac{21}{25}$ 6 $\frac{19}{20}$

7 Increase 470 by 10%.

8 20% of a sum of money is £5. What is the whole amount?

9 John spent 45% of his money. What percentage remained?

Which is the larger, and by how much:

10 $\frac{1}{5}$ of £6 or 25% of £6

11 $\frac{1}{20}$ of £100 or 4% of £100?

12 The label on a dress states that it is made of 100% Tricel. What does this mean?

13 A length of wool and nylon material contains 75% wool. What percentage of the material is nylon?

14 25% of a 10 kg bag of potatoes was bad. What mass of potatoes was sound?

Percentages

A

number tests		
date	items correct	possible score
2nd Sept.	35	50
23rd Sept.	19	25
16th Oct.	7	10
31st Oct.	11	20
10th Nov.	20	40

Find what part of the diagram is:

1 shaded ▓ 2 coloured ▢ 3 white □.

Express each answer in three ways:

4 as a fraction in its lowest terms

5 as a decimal fraction

6 as a percentage.

Express each of the following as a percentage.

7 $\frac{9}{100}$ 8 $\frac{7}{10}$ 9 0.07 10 0.6

The table shows Ian's scores in five number tests.

11 Find for each test what fraction of the total, in its lowest terms, he had correct.

On which date did he score:

12 the highest percentage

13 the lowest percentage?

14 On which dates did he score the same percentage?

B

When a shop has a sale, many goods are reduced in price.

January Sale
all prices reduced by 10%

usual prices			
socks	85p	cardigan	£7·90
gloves	£2·85	pullover	£6·35

Find:

1 the reduction in price of each article

2 the sale price of each article.

Restaurants often add a service charge of 10% to the cost of the meal.
Find the service charge and the total for each bill if the meal costs:

3 £1·50 4 £1·75 5 £0·65

6 £3·20 7 £10·10 8 £6·55.

At a concert, 10% of the people each paid 50p, 35% paid 30p and the remainder paid 20p.

9 What percentage paid 20p?

460 people attended the concert.

10 Find the number who paid each price.

11 Find the total amount collected.

C

Copy the table below and complete it.

100%	£1·00	1 m	1 kg	1 ℓ
1	75%	p	cm	g	mℓ
2	50%	p	cm	g	mℓ
3	25%	p	cm	g	mℓ
4	10%	p	cm	g	mℓ
5	5%	p	cm	g	mℓ
6	1%	p	cm	g	mℓ

Find the value of:

7 3% of £1·00   8 15% of £1·00

9 37% of £1·00   10 9% of £1·00

11 65% of 1 m   12 19% of 1 m

13 18% of 1 kg   14 7% of 1 kg

15 23% of 1 ℓ   16 52% of 1 ℓ.

What percentage of £1·00 is:

17 12p   18 33p   19 61p

20 90p   21 7½p   22 22½p?

What percentage of 1 metre is:

23 4 cm   24 13 cm   25 35.5 cm?

What percentage of 1 kg is:

26 20 g   27 60 g   28 150 g?

What percentage of 1 litre is:

29 200 mℓ   30 90 mℓ   31 300 mℓ?

Making sure

A

Multiply by 20.

1 46   **2** 54   **3** 38   **4** 17

Multiply by 30.

5 76   **6** 35.14   **7** £2·49   **8** £1·90

Multiply by 50.

9 5.186   **10** £10·11   **11** 16.034   **12** £0·53

Multiply by 90.

13 £1·62   **14** 3.74   **15** £5·37   **16** 0.25

Write the answers only.

17 £1·75 × 40   **18** £2·89 × 60   **19** £4·07 × 70

Write the answers to the following as £s.

20 25p × 80   **21** 36p × 40   **22** 19p × 60

There are no remainders in the following. Write the answers as decimals.

Divide by 10.

23 897   **24** 98.2   **25** 10.56   **26** 207

Divide by 20.

27 5950   **28** 9.5   **29** 642   **30** 16.96

Divide by 30.

31 57.0   **32** 8.4   **33** 4275   **34** 30.72

Write the answers only.

35 8950 ÷ 50   **36** 17.5 ÷ 70   **37** 204 ÷ 60

38 1512 ÷ 30   **39** £2·60 ÷ 20   **40** £19·50 ÷ 50

41 £8·00 ÷ 40   **42** £4·80 ÷ 30   **43** £10·50 ÷ 70

B

week ending	May 4	May 11	May 18	May 25	June 1
total weekly takings	£986	£1304	£1797	£1546	£1812

The table gives the gross takings in a shop for each of five weeks.

In which week were the takings

1 the highest   **2** the lowest?

3 Find the difference between these two amounts.

4 What was the total amount of money taken during the five weeks?

5 Find the average weekly takings.

6 Round off each of the weekly takings to the nearest hundred £s.

7 Check your answer to question **5** by finding an approximate average.

8 Draw a column graph to show the weekly takings to the nearest £10.
Mark the weeks on the horizontal axis.
Mark the £s on the vertical axis.

9 On the completed graph, draw a line to show the approximate average weekly takings to the nearest £10.

During which weeks were the takings

10 above the average   **11** below the average?

C

A boy describes a square as a shape with four equal sides.

1 Show, by a drawing, that his answer might be wrong.

2 Name the shape you have drawn.

Write these numbers.

3 $(3 \times 10^3) + (8 \times 10^2) + (6 \times 10^1) + (5 \times 1)$

4 $(9 \times 10^3) + (0 \times 10^2) + (0 \times 10^1) + (8 \times 1)$

David was born in 1973, Helen in 1974 and Andrew in 1975.

5 Find their average age in the year 2000.

6 Write the date of the second Thursday in March if the 1st March is on a Monday.

The drawing shows part of a Celsius thermometer.

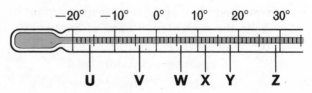

7 Write the temperature at each of the points marked **U**, **V**, **W**, **X**, **Y** and **Z**.

By how many degrees does the temperature rise or fall from:

8 **X** to **W**   **9** **Z** to **Y**   **10** **V** to **U**

11 **U** to **W**   **12** **X** to **V**   **13** **W** t

Sets

A

> **Remember**
>
> **A set is a collection of things.**
>
> These things can be numbers, letters, shapes, people or any kinds of objects which have something in common.

The things which belong to a set are called **members** of the set.

The members of a set are enclosed in **brackets** and are separated by **commas**.

A **capital letter** is used to name a set.

It is important to be able to describe a set accurately.

Example:

P = {13, 17, 19}

P = {prime numbers between 12 and 20}.

1 In this way, describe the following sets.

F = {5, 10, 15, 20, 25, 30}

X = {4, 36, 16, 25, 9}

B = {$\frac{3}{5}$, $\frac{1}{5}$, $\frac{4}{5}$, $\frac{2}{5}$}

L = {km, cm, mm, m}

2 Use brackets and list members of each of these sets.

H = {odd numbers between 88 and 100}

M = {multiples of 4 between 71 and 81}

Q = {names of four quadrilaterals}

G = {factors of 24 greater than 3}

Z = {multiples of 6 between 17 and 61}

B The table shows the names of the children who have a birthday in the autumn term.

Sept.	Oct.	Nov.	Dec.
Jane	Peter	Ann	
Mary	Jill	Susan	
John		Tom	
Tony			
Paul			

1 Write, in brackets, the members of S = {children with a September birthday}. The first letter of the month has been used to name the set.

2 In the same way, name and write the members of the set of children whose birthdays are in each of the other months.

As no child in the class has a birthday in December, Set D is an **empty set** and is written { } or by using the symbol $\emptyset$.

3 Write: D = { } or D = $\emptyset$.

4 From the following sets, choose the empty sets and write them in two ways.

X = {multiples of 8 less than 7}

P = {factors of 9 greater than 10}

Z = {square numbers greater than 100}

F = {fractions greater than $\frac{99}{100}$}

T = {prime numbers between 90 and 96}

R = {triangles with two obtuse angles}

C

1 Some sets have few, one or no members. Write the members of each of these sets.

W = {multiples of 9 between 10 and 19}

B = {odd numbers divisible by 4}

H = {multiples of 7 between 8 and 25}

Some sets have a large number of members, e.g.

C = {children who attend your school}

K = {fractions less than $\frac{1}{2}$}

M = {multiples of 5 and 10}

E = {whole numbers less than 1000}.

Choose and describe these sets.

2 any three sets with no members

3 any three sets with one member

4 any three sets with few members

5 any three sets with many members

6 Give a reason why it is impossible to list all the members of the following sets.

S = {even numbers greater than 100}

T = {fractions equal to $\frac{2}{5}$}

Y = {decimal fractions smaller than 0.01}

Sets

A When writing the members of a set with a large number of members, a short method is used.
For example:

$P=\{1, \ 2, \ 3, \ . \ . \ . \ 12, \ 13, \ 14\}$.

The three dots stand for
4, 5, 6, 7, 8, 9, 10, 11.

1 What do the dots stand for in each of the following sets?

$H=\{5, \ 10, \ 15, \ 20, \ . \ . \ . \ 55, \ 60\}$

$F=\{3, \ 3\frac{3}{4}, \ 4\frac{1}{2}, \ 5\frac{1}{4}, \ . \ . \ . \ 11\frac{1}{4}, \ 12\}$

$A=\{a, \ b, \ c, \ d, \ . \ . \ . \ x, \ y, \ z\}$

2 Using dots, write the members of these sets.

$N=\{\text{page numbers in this book}\}$

$K=\{\text{multiples of 6 less than 70}\}$

$D=\{\text{multiples of 10 between 79 and 199}\}$

Some sets have an infinite (unlimited) number of members, in which case the three dots are placed as shown in the example below.

$B=\{\text{whole numbers greater than 500}\}$

$B=\{501, \ 502, \ 503, \ 504, \ . \ . \ .\}$

3 In this way, write the members of the following sets.

$T=\{\text{multiples of 7}\}$

$M=\{\text{even numbers greater than 100}\}$

$S=\{\text{square numbers}\}$

$O=\{\text{odd numbers greater than 50}\}$

$C=\{\text{numbers exactly divisible by 9}\}$

$P=\{\text{numbers greater than 10 ending in 1}\}$

4 Describe three sets each of which has an infinite number of members.

5 Using dots, write the members of each set.

B

$\in$ stands for **'is a member of'** or **'are members of'**.

$\notin$ stands for **'is not a member of'** or **'are not members of'**.

1 Write and complete the following, using the symbols $\in$ or $\notin$ in place of $\bullet$.

rectangle $\bullet$ $\{$quadrilaterals$\}$

acute angles $\bullet$ $\{$angles greater than 90°$\}$

XI $\bullet$ $\{$Roman numerals less than XX$\}$

$\frac{18}{24}$ $\bullet$ $\{$fractions equal to $\frac{3}{4}$$\}$

D $\bullet$ $\{$Roman numerals$\}$

$\frac{9}{16}$ $\bullet$ $\{$fractions less than $\frac{1}{2}$$\}$

sphere $\bullet$ $\{$prisms$\}$

Using the symbol $\notin$, write the members which you think do not belong in each of these sets. Give a reason for your choice. The first is done for you.

$F=\{1, \ 3, \ 5, \ 7, \ 9, \ 10\}$
$10 \notin F$. 1, 3, 5, 7, 9 are all odd numbers.

2 $N=\{9, \ 18, \ 27, \ 35, \ 36\}$

3 $P=\{3, \ 7, \ 9, \ 11, \ 13\}$

4 Write the members of these sets.

$Y=\{\text{even numbers between 0 and 19}\}$

$Z=\{\text{multiples of 2 between 0 and 19}\}$

Notice that sets Y and Z have the same members.
They are equal or identical sets.

Equal or **identical** sets are shown by the sign $=$ e.g. set Y$=$set Z   or   Y$=$Z.

5 Write the members of these sets.

$V=\{\text{even numbers between 9 and 11}\}$

$W=\{\text{prime numbers between 2 and 8}\}$

$T=\{\text{multiples of 3 between 13 and 16}\}$

$X=\{\text{whole numbers between 14 and 16}\}$

$U=\{\text{odd numbers between 2 and 8}\}$

$A=\{\text{multiples of 5 between 9 and 12}\}$

6 From the sets V, W, T, X, U and A write three pairs of identical sets.

Remember Members of identical sets need not be in the same order. When sets are **not** identical, the sign $\neq$ is used.

Angles

A You have learned previously that **angles** measure turns or **rotations**.

> ### A complete turn is 4 right angles or 360°.

A turn or rotation can be in either a **clockwise** or an **anticlockwise** direction.

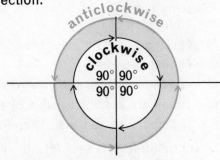

How many right angles are there in:

1 ½ turn   2 ¼ turn   3 ¾ turn?

How many degrees are there in:

4 2 right angles or a straight angle

5 3 right angles   6 ½ right angle

7 ⅓ right angle   8 ⅔ right angle?

9 Write in degrees the size of the angles which can be measured with a pair of set squares (a 45° and a 60° set square).

In each of the drawings below, the angles at the centre are of equal size.

10 How many degrees are there in each angle in diagrams **e, f, g** and **h**?

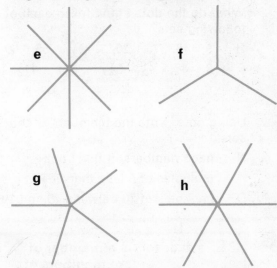

B

> ### Angles are named according to their size.

An arrow marks each of the named angles. It also tells you the direction of the rotation.

In which of the angles below is the rotation **1** clockwise   **2** anticlockwise?

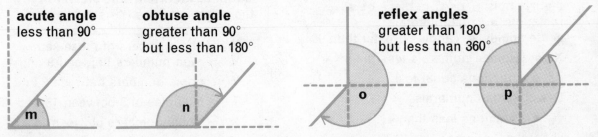

acute angle
less than 90°

obtuse angle
greater than 90°
but less than 180°

reflex angles
greater than 180°
but less than 360°

3 Find the number of degrees in each angle below marked with a letter.

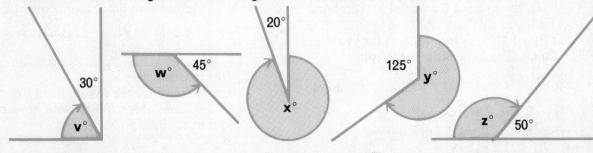

Angles direction

A Look at each of these angles marked with an arrow.
Write the letters which show angles between:

1 0° and 90°   2 90° and 180°   3 180° and 270°   4 270° and 360°.

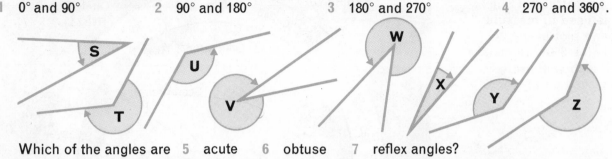

Which of the angles are   5 acute   6 obtuse   7 reflex angles?

B Stand facing north.

Through how many degrees do you turn clockwise from north to face:

1 east   2 south

3 west?

Through how many degrees do you turn anticlockwise from north to face:

4 east   5 south   6 west?

Through how many degrees do you turn in moving clockwise from:

7 N to NE   8 S to SE   9 W to NW?

10 Draw this table.

directions from	degrees clockwise	degrees anti-clockwise	total degrees
N to SE			
E to SW			
S to NE			
W to SE			
SE to SW			
NW to NE			

11 Fill in the number of degrees clockwise and anticlockwise between the given directions.

12 In each case, add together the two measurements.

13 Each total should be 360°. Give the reason.

C There are no roads or signposts to guide ships and aircraft to their destinations. The captain has to steer his craft on its **course** by finding a **bearing** which is the **angle in degrees from north turning clockwise.**

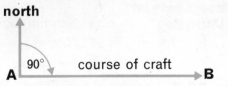

The diagram shows the course **A** to **B** in which the captain steers his craft.

1 Write: a the bearing
            b the compass direction.

Write   a the bearing   b the compass direction from **A** to **B** in each diagram.

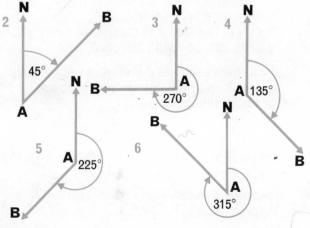

Bearings

An instrument which is used to measure and plot bearings is the 360° protractor which is shown placed on the map.

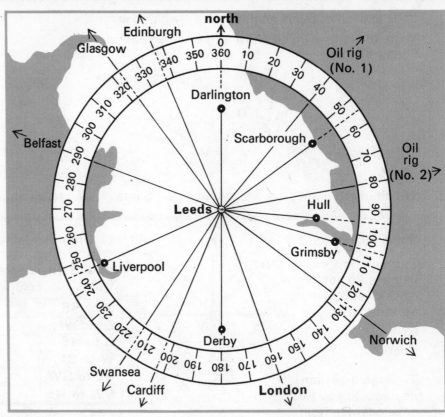

The protractor is placed in position so that all the bearings are read from **Leeds** which is in the **centre** and from which the **north line** is drawn.

First look for the following places and their directions from Leeds. Then read the bearing of each off the protractor.

1 Darlington   2 Oil rig No. 1
3 Oil rig No. 2   4 London
5 Derby   6 Belfast

7 Which town is due north of Leeds?
8 Which town is due south of Leeds?

Look at the protractor again.
You will see that it is marked at every 10°.
0°, 10°, 20°, ... 340°, 350°, 360° or 0°

You must estimate therefore, as accurately as you can, the bearings which come between the divisions.

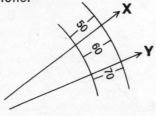

In the example, bearing **X** is 54° approximately, bearing **Y** is 68° approximately.

Now read and estimate the approximate bearing from Leeds to:

9 Scarborough   10 Hull
11 Grimsby   12 Norwich
13 Cardiff   14 Swansea
15 Liverpool   16 Glasgow
17 Edinburgh.

Which of the towns are approximately the following compass directions from Leeds?

18 E   19 SE   20 SW   21 NW

Measure the distances on the map in mm from Leeds to:

22 Darlington   23 Scarborough
24 Hull   25 Grimsby
26 Derby   27 Liverpool.

The map is drawn to a scale:
1 mm to 3 km.

28 Use this scale to find the approximate distance in km from Leeds to each of the six towns.

Puzzle corner

A

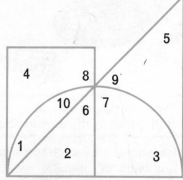

In the diagram there is a triangle, a rectangle and a semicircle.

Find the numbers which are in:
1. the triangle only
2. the triangle and the semicircle only
3. the rectangle and the semicircle only
4. the triangle, the rectangle and the semicircle.
5. 90p is made up of an equal number of FIVES, pennies, TENS and TWOS. Find the number of each of the coins.

B

The sum of four numbers is 30. When the four numbers are arranged in order, smallest first, each is twice the number before it.
1. Find the four numbers.

The diameter of a penny is 20.3 mm.

Find:
2. the length and the width in mm of a rectangle into which 20 pennies can be fitted as shown in the diagram
3. the perimeter of the rectangle in cm.
4. Find the total of:
1^2, 2^2, 3^2, 4^2, 5^2 and 6^2.
5. Father gives John a TWO each time Rachel has a FIVE. If Rachel receives 60p altogether, how much does John receive?

C

1. On paper, draw and cut out a square of 5 cm side and a rectangle 8 cm by 5 cm.
2. Cut the rectangle along a diagonal to make two triangles.
3. Use the square and the two triangles to make a trapezium. Stick it on paper.
4. Find in mm the perimeter of the trapezium.

Helen spent $\frac{1}{2}$ of her savings on a present, $\frac{1}{2}$ of what was left on a book and $\frac{1}{2}$ of the remainder on sweets.
5. What fraction of her savings had she left?
6. If she had £1·60 in the first place, how much did she spend on each item?

D

James counted 50 picture cards in 30 seconds or $\frac{1}{2}$ minute.

Write and complete:
1. 100 cards are counted in ☐ min
2. 1000 cards are counted in ☐ min
3. 10 000 cards are counted in ☐ min.
4. At this rate, how many minutes would it take James to count non-stop 1 million cards?
5. Find how many days, hours and minutes it would take him.

A secret code is made by numbering the letters of the alphabet.
A is 26, B is 25, C is 24, and so on.
6. Write the answer in code to this question.
4 19 26 7   18 8   2 12 6 9
21 12 9 22 13 26 14 22?
7. Travelling at a speed of 90 km/h, a journey takes 2 hours. How long will the journey take travelling at a speed of 60 km/h?

Surfaces and solids

A

 R S  T U  V

W

Look at these pictures of common things, each of which is a solid.

1 How many surfaces has each solid?

2 These surfaces are either flat or curved. Write two members of each of these sets.
F = {solids with flat surfaces only}
C = {solids with curved surfaces only}
Z = {solids with flat and curved surfaces}

A flat surface is called a **plane** surface.

How many plane surfaces has:
3 a sheet of paper   4 a brick
5 the outside of a box without a lid?

Plane surfaces can be horizontal, vertical or oblique.

The drawing shows a garage with the door and window open.

How many of the outside surfaces are:
6 horizontal   7 vertical   8 oblique?

B

The walls of a building are usually vertical.

To test them a builder uses a plumb-line.

1 Make a plumb-line and test surfaces in the class-room which you think are vertical.

Floors, shelves, etc, must be horizontal, so the builder uses a spirit-level.

2 Find out how to make a spirit-level from a bottle almost filled with water.

3 Use it to test floors, desk and table-tops and other surfaces you think are horizontal.

C

a   b   c   d   e   f

u   v   w   x   y   z

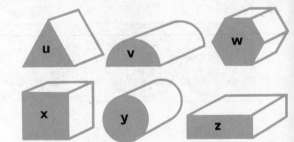

Surfaces have **two dimensions**, length and breadth.
They have no thickness or height.

1 Write the name of each plane surface shown above.

Solids have **three dimensions**, length, breadth and thickness or height.

2 Match each solid above (**u** to **z**) with one of the plane surfaces (**a** to **f**).

Remember	**Lines** have length only, **one dimension.**
	Surfaces have length and breadth, **two dimensions.**
	Solids have length, breadth and thickness, **three dimensions.**

Surfaces measuring area

A

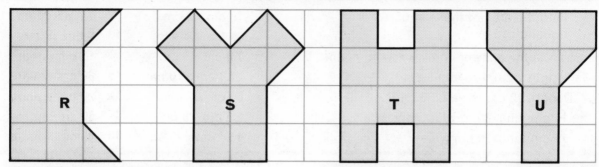

The amount of surface in a shape is called its **area**.

The area of a surface is measured in equal squares.

Square centimetres (cm²) are used when measurements are given in cm.

Look at the shapes **R**, **S**, **T** and **U** above.

By counting the equal squares, find which shape has:

1 the largest area   2 the smallest area.

3 Which shapes have the same area?

The squares which cover the surface of each shape are cm².
Measure some of them to make sure.

4 Write the area of each shape in cm².

B   Areas of squares and rectangles

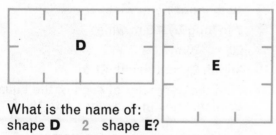

What is the name of:

1 shape **D**   2 shape **E**?

The perimeter of each shape has been marked off in cm.

3 Find the perimeter of each shape.

4 Draw the shapes **D** and **E** on cm squared paper.

How many cm² are there in a row:

5 in shape **D**   6 in shape **E**?

How many rows of cm² are there:

7 in shape **D**   8 in shape **E**?

9 Find the area of each shape.
Check the answers by counting the cm².

Write and complete:

10 **rectangle D**   length   = □ cm
                      breadth   = □ cm
   area   = (□ × □) cm² = □ cm²

11 **square E**   length   = □ cm
                     breadth   = □ cm
   area   = (□ × □) cm² = □ cm².

Find the area of the squares or rectangles below by writing out each example as in **B10** or **B11**.

12 length 5 cm   breadth 3 cm

13 length 9 cm   breadth 6 cm

14 8 cm long by 4 cm wide

15 7 cm long by 7 cm wide

16 4 cm long by 4 cm wide

17 Check the answers **B12** to **B16** by drawing the shapes on cm squared paper and counting the squares.

18 Find the perimeter of each of the shapes **B12** to **B16**.

From the examples above, you learn that
Area = number of units in the length × number of units in the breadth or width.
This is usually written for short as a formula: **A = l × b**   or   **A = lb**.

Area squares and rectangles

A Find the area of these squares or rectangles.

Write the answers only when you can.

1 length 7 cm, breadth 5 cm
2 length 12 cm, breadth 9 cm
3 14 cm long, 8 cm wide
4 17 cm long, 10 cm wide

5 18 cm × 6 cm
6 35 cm × 30 cm
7 7.8 cm × 5 cm
8 27.8 cm × 10 cm
9 50 cm × 20 cm
10 2.5 cm × 8 cm
11 18.5 cm × 16 cm

12 7 cm square
13 9 cm square
14 15 cm square
15 30 cm square
16 20 cm square
17 50 cm square
18 45 cm square

B Square metres

When the measurements of larger surfaces are given in **metres**, the areas are measured in **square metres** m^2.

1 Spread sheets of newspaper on the floor so that they overlap and form a square.

2 Adjust the sheets of paper until you estimate that each side of the square is 1 metre long.

3 Now measure the sides and make them exactly 1 metre long.

4 What is the area covered by newspaper?

5 Name a surface in the class-room which is approximately 1 m^2.

Find the area in m^2 of each of the following squares or rectangles.
6 length 12 m, breadth 6 m
7 16 m long, 1.5 m wide
8 7 m long by 4.5 m wide
9 20 m × 20 m
10 length 21 m, breadth 21 m
11 Find the perimeter of each of the squares or rectangles in questions **6** to **10**.

C The drawing shows the area and the length of a rectangle.

1 Which measurement is not shown?

area 21 cm²

|← 7 cm →|

2 How many cm² are there in the area?
3 How many centimetre squares are there in each row?
4 How many rows of centimetre squares are required to make 21 altogether?
5 What is the breadth of the rectangle?

Find each missing measurement.

	6	7	8	9	10
length	11.5 m	13 m		50 m	
breadth	9 m		8 m		8.6 m
area		104 m²	68 m²	500 m²	86 m²

Write and complete each formula below.
Use:
A for the number of units in the area,
l for the number of units in the length,
b for the number of units in the breadth.

11 $A = \square \times \square$

12 perimeter $= 2(\square + \square)$

13 $\dfrac{A}{l} = \square$

14 $\dfrac{A}{b} = \square$

Area   squares and rectangles

A Measure, to the nearest cm, the length and breadth of:
1 the front cover of this book
2 three sheets of paper of different sizes
3 a sheet of newspaper.

4 Now find the area of each in cm².

Measure, to the nearest m, the length and the width of:
5 the class-room
6 the school corridor
7 the kitchen and living-room at home.

8 Now find the area of each in m².

B A rectangle measures 12 cm by 7.5 cm.
1 Find its area.
2 If the length and the width of the rectangle were doubled, what would be the area?

Pieces of card are cut in three sizes, the smallest being 18 cm by 13.5 cm. The measurement of the length and breadth increases by 2.5 cm for each size.
3 Write the dimensions of the other two sizes.
4 Find the area of each of the three sizes.
5 Find the difference in area of a square of 9 cm side and a square of 10 cm side.

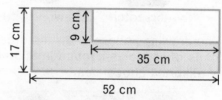

Use the given dimensions to find:
6 the area of the shaded part
7 the perimeter of the shaded part.

8 A rectangle measures 14 cm by 12 cm. What is the width of a rectangle of the same area if its length is 16 cm?

9 How many squares of 2 cm side can be cut from a square of 10 cm side?

C

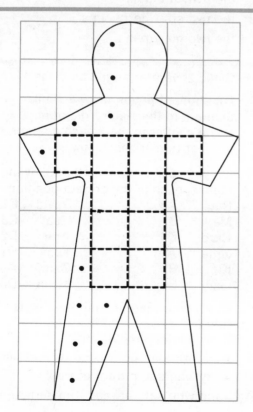

The felt toy pattern has been drawn on cm squared paper.
1 To find the approximate area of the pattern count the whole squares.
2 Count as whole squares also those which **are a half or more** (some of these have been marked with a dot).
Do not count the squares which are less than a half.
How many part squares are counted as whole ones?
3 What is the approximate area in cm² of the pattern?
4 Write the dimensions of the smallest area of felt from which the pattern can be cut.
5 Approximately how many cm² of felt will be wasted?

To make the toy, two shapes must be cut, one for the front, the other for the back. What length of felt will be needed if it is:
6 10 cm wide   7 6 cm wide?

Fixing position

A

coffee cream   liquid cherry   caramel   marzipan

butterscotch   strawberry cup

The drawings above show the different kinds of chocolates found in this box of assorted chocolates.

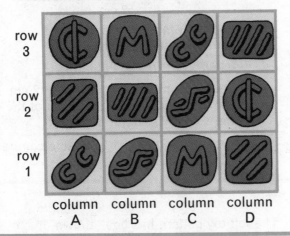

row 3

row 2

row 1

column A   column B   column C   column D

The chocolates are placed in columns and in rows.

How many:

1 columns are there   2 rows are there?

You will see that each column has a letter and each row has a number.

> **Notice that the letters and numbers start from the bottom left-hand corner.**

3 Find the butterscotch in column B.
In which row is it?
This position is written B2.

4 Find the butterscotch in column D.
In which row is it?
This position is written D3.

In the same way,
writing first the letter of the column and then the number of the row, give the positions of:

5 the two coffee creams

6 the two liquid cherries

7 the two caramels

8 the two strawberry cups

9 the two marzipans.

B

The children in class 1 are arranged in columns and in rows as shown.

4	Perry	Dawn	Mark	Denise
3	June	Gary	Julie	Paul
2	John	Sally	Craig	Helen
1	Anita	Peter	Diane	Ian
	A	B	C	D

Write the positions of the following children. Write the letter of the column first and then the number of the row.

1 Sally   2 Paul   3 Diane   4 Perry

Write the names of the children in each of the following positions.

5 B4   6 A2   7 D4

8 C3   9 B1   10 C2

11 D1   12 B3   13 A1

14 C4   15 A3   16 D2

Class 2 were arranged as class 1.

17 On squared paper, draw a similar diagram to the class 1 diagram.
Write a letter to mark each column and a number to mark each row.

18 On your diagram, write the following names, each in the correct position.

Paul	A3		David	C1
Mark	B1		Lisa	C3
Carol	D4		Ann	D2
Jane	A1		Tom	D1
Kim	B2		Gail	A4
Gary	C4		Kevin	D3

Study your diagram and then write first the column and then the row to show the positions of:

19 Peter who sat between Paul and Lisa

20 Mary who sat in front of Paul

21 John who sat between Kim and Ann.

Fixing position

A At the Summer Fair, Sarah and Peter arranged a competition called **'Hunt the Treasure'**.

They drew a grid on a large sheet of paper and numbered the **lines across from 1 to 10** and the **lines up from 1 to 8**.

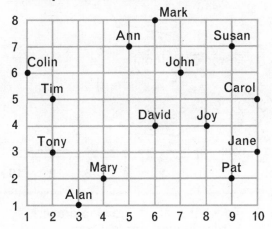

Children guessed at which point the treasure was hidden. For example:

Mary chose 4 across and 2 up or 4,2.

John's choice was 7,6.

Remember that the number across is always written first.

Write the pair of numbers which gives the position chosen by each of these children.

1 Tony   2 Alan   3 Tim   4 Colin

5 Ann   6 Joy   7 Susan   8 Jane

9 Mark   10 Pat   11 David   12 Carol

Obtain a sheet of paper ruled in large squares.

13 Draw a grid like the one in the diagram and number the lines across and up in the same way.

14 From your answers to **A1-12**, mark in the points which have already been chosen.

15 Check their positions from the diagram.

16 Now mark in these positions.
Terry 8,7   Helen 4,6   James 8,8
Trudy 6,5   Charles 6,1   Perry 10,8

17 Sarah and Peter had fixed the point 8,2 as the position of the treasure.

Name the child who won the competition by being the nearest.

B The map showing several imaginary roads and places has been drawn on a grid.

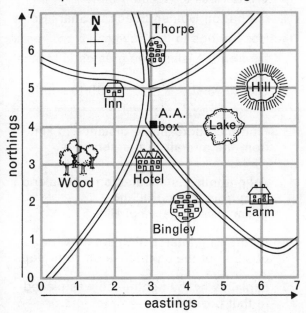

The numbers **across the bottom** starting from 0 are from west to east and are called **eastings**.

1 The numbers **up the side** starting from 0 are called **northings**. Why is this so?

Write the position of:

2 the village of Thorpe

3 the village of Bingley   4 the hotel

5 the A.A. box   6 the hill   7 the wood

8 the lake   9 the inn   10 the farm.

11 What is the position of the crossroads south of Thorpe?

Write the direction of:

12 the hill from the farm

13 the inn from the village of Thorpe.

Which of the villages is nearer to:

14 the inn   15 the hotel?

Fixing position

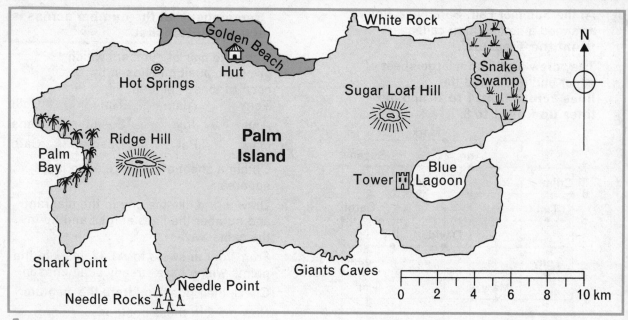

A This is a map of Palm Island.

Write the names of marked places which are situated on or near:

1 the north coast   2 the east coast

3 the south coast   4 the west coast.

Needle Point is approximately SW of Sugar Loaf Hill.

What is the approximate direction from:

5 Ridge Hill to Palm Bay

6 the hut on Golden Beach to the tower near the Blue Lagoon

7 Shark Point to Ridge Hill

8 Giants Caves to Hot Springs?

9 To what scale is the map drawn? Write: Scale 1 cm to ☐km.

Find the actual distance represented on the map by:

10 4 cm   11 0.5 cm   12 6.5 cm

13 1 mm   14 7 mm   15 15 mm.

By measuring and using the scale, find the actual distance 'as the crow flies' from

16 White Rock to Needle Point

17 the hut on Golden Beach to Shark Point

18 Hot Springs to the Tower.

Find on the island the greatest distance from:

19 east to west   20 north to south.

B

1 Using tracing paper, draw an outline of the island.

2 Mark the positions of Sugar Loaf Hill, Ridge Hill, White Rock and Needle Point.

3 A wrecked aircraft was sighted due south of White Rock and due east of Ridge Hill. Mark its position.

4 Survivors were seen north of Needle Point and west of Sugar Loaf Hill. Mark their position.

5 Find the approximate distance in km from the aircraft to the survivors.

A lighthouse is situated on a headland 7 km from Ridge Hill and 15 km from Sugar Loaf Hill.

6 By drawing intersecting arcs, fix the position of the lighthouse on your map.

7 Explain why the lighthouse was placed in that position.

Making sure

A

1 Write in brackets the members of these sets.

N={multiples of 8 between 23 and 75}
F={factors of 48 less than 10}
C={cubic numbers less than 130}

A car travels at an average speed of 80 km/h.

2 How far does it travel in 75 min?

3 How long will it take to travel 200 km?

The radius of a circle measures 4.5 cm.

4 Find its circumference to the nearest mm. (π=3.14)

5 Draw a triangle, base 78 mm and the other two sides each 62 mm.

6 Name the triangle according to its sides.

7 Draw and measure its height in mm.

8 Divide £6·10 by 19. Give the answer to the nearest penny.

9 By how many twelfths is $\frac{5}{6} > \frac{3}{4}$?

10 What must be added to $83\frac{1}{2}$p to make a total of £1·35?

11 How many degrees below boiling-point is a temperature of 68.3°C?

12 Write in degrees Celsius, the temperature which is 7.4°C below freezing-point.

B

The graph shows the rainfall at a seaside resort for eight months of the year.

During which months was the rainfall

1 the highest   2 the lowest?

3 Draw and complete this table.

month	Mar.	Apr.	May	June	July	Aug.	Sept.	Oct.
rainfall in mm								

4 Find the average monthly rainfall.

During which month was the rainfall:

5 average   6 above average   7 below average?

Find out how rainfall is measured. If possible, use a rain-gauge and in the same way, record what you find and make a graph.

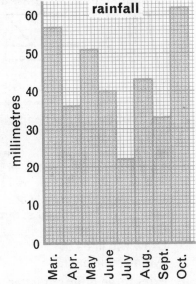

rainfall

millimetres

Mar. Apr. May June July Aug. Sept. Oct.

C

Copy and complete this chart.

per cent	decimal	fraction hundredths	fraction lowest terms
1 5%	☐	$\frac{☐}{100}$	☐
2 ☐%	☐	$\frac{☐}{100}$	$\frac{4}{25}$
3 ☐%	0.4	$\frac{☐}{100}$	☐
4 ☐%		$\frac{26}{100}$	☐
5 8%	☐	$\frac{☐}{100}$	☐
6 ☐%	☐	$\frac{66}{100}$	☐
7 ☐%	0.95	$\frac{☐}{100}$	☐

Find:

8 75% of 20 kg   9 90% of 20 kg
10 76% of 50 ℓ   11 52% of 25 m.

Set down and work the following.

12 870÷29   13 936÷18   14 806÷31

15 Find the missing measurements.

rectangle	W	X	Y	Z
length		15 cm	2.75 m	
breadth	7 cm		2 m	4 cm
area	91 cm²	375 cm²		
perimeter				24 cm

Symmetry

Shapes which balance about a line are called **symmetrical shapes**.
The **balance line** is called a **line of symmetry**.

A line of symmetry divides a shape into two congruent parts.

When a symmetrical shape is folded along a line of symmetry,
one half will fit exactly over the other.

A The shapes below are symmetrical. Copy them on squared paper and then draw the line of symmetry in each. The first example has been done for you.

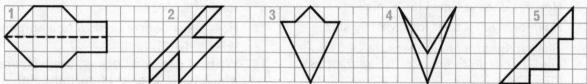

The following are **half shapes** and a line of symmetry in each is shown by a dotted line. On squared paper, draw and complete each symmetrical shape.

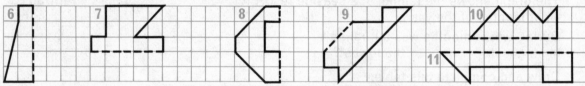

B Each of the printed capital letters below is symmetrical.

M K T C

1 Copy them accurately and draw a line of vertical or horizontal symmetry in each.

2 Copy these letters. Draw two lines of symmetry in each.

X H

3 Print three different letters each of which has no line of symmetry.

Remember Lines of symmetry can be horizontal, vertical or oblique.

Draw these shapes on squared paper. Show, by dotted lines, two lines of symmetry in each.

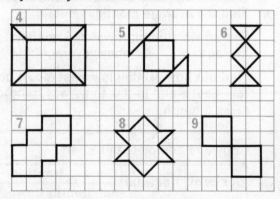

C Look at these drawings of space satellites. Which of them are symmetrical?

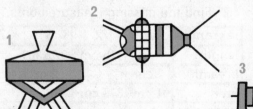

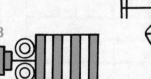

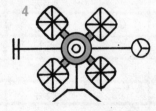

Symmetry

A Look at the shapes below.

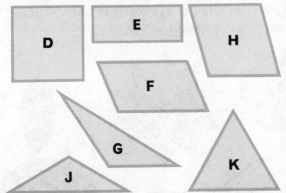

1 Write the letter and name of each quadrilateral.

Name each triangle by:
2 its sides   3 its angles.

How many lines of symmetry are there in:
4 a square   5 a rectangle
6 a parallelogram   7 a rhombus
8 an isosceles triangle
9 a scalene triangle
10 an equilateral triangle?
11 Mark your answers to **A4** to **10**.
12 If you have made any mistakes, draw the shapes making each side twice the length of those in the diagram.
13 Then, by cutting and folding, find the number of lines of symmetry.

B
1 Draw a large circle and cut it out.

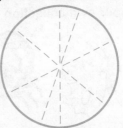

2 Try to discover, by folding, how many lines of symmetry there are in a circle.
3 Do all the lines of symmetry pass though the centre?
4 What special name is given to each line of symmetry in a circle?
5 Draw another large circle and construct a regular hexagon by stepping off the radius round the circumference.

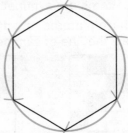

6 Cut out the hexagon and show by dotted lines the number of lines of symmetry.

C Write the letters of the shapes below which have:
1 no line of symmetry   2 one line of symmetry
3 two lines of symmetry   4 three or more lines of symmetry.

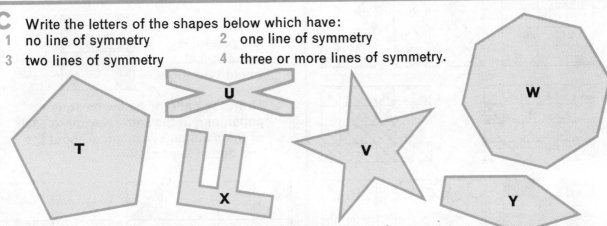

5 Now trace the shapes which have more than two lines of symmetry.
6 Cut out the shapes and find, by folding, how many lines of symmetry there are in each.

Symmetry

A The shapes of many things in nature and also of many man-made things are symmetrical. The drawings show a few examples. Look for a line or lines of symmetry in each shape. Make your own collection of pictures and drawings of symmetrical shapes.

B Many patterns are symmetrical.

Copy these patterns on squared paper and draw the line of symmetry in each.

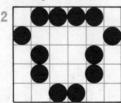

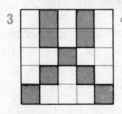

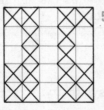

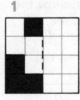

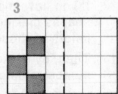

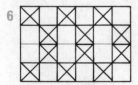

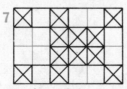

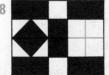

C Each of the drawings below is half of a symmetrical pattern.

Each line of symmetry is shown by a dotted line.

Draw and complete each pattern on squared paper.

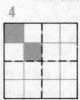

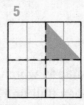

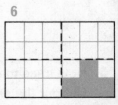

In this example, the pattern is symmetrical about **two lines**.

Draw the patterns below on squared paper, and in the same way make each of the patterns symmetrical about the two dotted lines shown.

Decimal fractions

A Write as decimals.

1 $3\frac{8}{10}$ 2 $40\frac{6}{10}$ 3 $109\frac{5}{10}$

4 47 tenths 5 72 tenths 6 50 tenths

7 125 tenths 8 206 tenths 9 401 tenths

10 $\frac{48}{100}$ 11 $\frac{90}{100}$ 12 $\frac{4}{100}$

13 $1\frac{15}{100}$ 14 $10\frac{1}{100}$ 15 $120\frac{66}{100}$

16 52 hundredths 17 70 hundredths

18 630 hundredths 19 209 hundredths

Multiply by 10.

20 3.6 21 2.17 22 0.28 23 90.06

Divide by 10.

24 7 25 118 26 120.5 27 19.04

Multiply by 100.

28 0.3 29 20.7 30 3.45 31 7.01

32 0.006 33 0.025 34 3.125 35 50.805

Divide by 100.

36 3 37 6 38 7185 39 402

40 900 41 2407 42 24 43 160

Write as decimals.

44 $\frac{359}{1000}$ 45 $\frac{47}{1000}$ 46 $\frac{8}{1000}$

47 $6\frac{125}{1000}$ 48 $8\frac{204}{1000}$ 49 $9\frac{2}{1000}$

50 $25\frac{15}{1000}$ 51 $30\frac{110}{1000}$ 52 $420\frac{30}{1000}$

53 17 thousandths 54 803 thousandths

55 2 thousandths 56 418 thousandths

57 1365 thousandths 58 7504 thousandths

59 4660 thousandths 60 8005 thousandths

Multiply by 1000.

61 0.248 62 0.065 63 0.009 64 0.5

65 0.12 66 0.307 67 3.6 68 21.31

69 73.2 70 10.01 71 4.255 72 8.004

Divide by 1000.

73 4 74 28 75 36 76 70

77 120 78 192 79 605 80 1240

81 6381 82 5508 83 1100 84 99 457

B Write and complete:

1 $4.3 = 4 + \frac{\square}{10} = \frac{\square}{10}$

2 $72.1 = \square\,\text{tens} + \square\,\text{units} + \frac{\square}{10} = \square\,\text{units} + \frac{\square}{10}$

3 $50.6 = \square\,\text{tens} + \frac{\square}{10} = \frac{\square}{10}$

4 $225.5 = \square\,\text{hundreds} + \square\,\text{tens} + \square\,\text{units} + \frac{\square}{10}$
$= \square\,\text{units} + \frac{\square}{10} = \frac{\square}{10}$

5 $0.83 = \frac{\square}{10} + \frac{\square}{100} = \frac{\square}{100}$

6 $0.697 = \frac{\square}{10} + \frac{\square}{100} + \frac{\square}{1000} = \frac{\square}{100} + \frac{\square}{1000}$
$= \frac{\square}{1000}$

7 $6.108 = \square\,\text{units} + \frac{\square}{10} + \frac{\square}{100} + \frac{\square}{1000}$
$= \frac{\square}{10} + \frac{\square}{1000} = \frac{\square}{1000}$

8 $9.004 = \square\,\text{units} + \frac{\square}{1000} = \frac{\square}{1000}.$

Change to vulgar fractions in their lowest terms.

9 0.5 10 0.18 11 0.05 12 0.375

13 0.6 14 0.005 15 0.625 16 0.25

17 0.02 18 0.125 19 0.025 20 0.75

Write these numbers, putting in a decimal point to make the 5 have a value of 5 hundredths.

21 1025 22 3150 23 59 24 580

C Write the answers only.

1 $1 - 0.1$ 2 $1 - 0.01$ 3 $1 - 0.001$

4 $3 - 0.75$ 5 $4 - 0.23$ 6 $7 - 0.09$

7 $6 - 0.008$ 8 $8 - 0.125$ 9 $9 - 0.375$

10 $5 - 0.076$ 11 $2 - 0.011$ 12 $4 - 0.235$

13 $4.25 + 1.7$ 14 $6.9 + 2.11$ 15 $5.06 + 0.8$

16 $8.05 + 0.25$ 17 $7.27 + 1.3$ 18 $2.88 + 2.2$

19 $3.006 + 0.05$ 20 $1.9 + 0.001$ 21 $0.55 + 0.05$

22 $0.025 + 0.75$ 23 $4.1 + 0.99$ 24 $2.22 + 0.006$

25 1.8×7 26 3.45×8 27 1.99×9

28 3.062×4 29 5.014×6 30 2.325×5

31 5.553×2 32 0.754×3 33 3.108×9

34 $7.84 \div 7$ 35 $1.55 \div 5$ 36 $6.096 \div 3$

37 $2.64 \div 8$ 38 $0.042 \div 7$ 39 $10.06 \div 2$

40 $0.40 \div 5$ 41 $12.0 \div 8$ 42 $5.0 \div 4$

Multiply by 10, by 100, by 1000.

43 2.725 ℓ 44 6.23 m 45 1.2 kg

Divide by 10, by 100.

46 £4·50 47 50.0 m 48 12.5 ℓ

Divide by 1000.

49 50 ℓ 50 176 m 51 2 kg

Measuring angles 180° protractor

A Which of these angles do you estimate is **1** 90° **2** 45° **3** 30° **4** 60° **5** 150° **6** 120°?

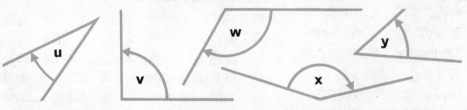

7 Use the angles on the set squares to check your answers.

In which of the angles is the rotation shown by the arrows:

8 clockwise   **9** anticlockwise?

10 Which of the following angles cannot be drawn or measured using the angles on the set squares?

135°   50°   95°

75°   126°   105°

B The 180° protractor is usually used to measure angles in degrees.

Make and learn to use the simple protractor shown in the diagram.

1 On stiff paper or thin card, draw and cut out a semicircle of 45 mm radius.

2 Mark the centre.

3 Fit the semicircle into the diagram.

Keep the baselines level, with one centre point over the other, as in the diagram.

4 Mark the division points round the edge, and draw lines towards the centre as shown.

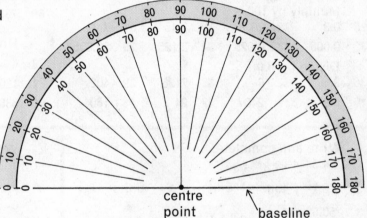

centre point

baseline

5 Number each division line carefully.

6 How many degrees are there in each division?

7 Up to how many degrees will the protractor measure?

C **To measure angles in a clockwise direction**

1 Place the protractor on the angle so that the centre point is exactly on **V** (the vertex of the angle) and the baseline is exactly over one arm of the angle.

Read from the scale on the protractor the number of degrees in

2 the acute angle **AVC**

3 the obtuse angle **AVT**.

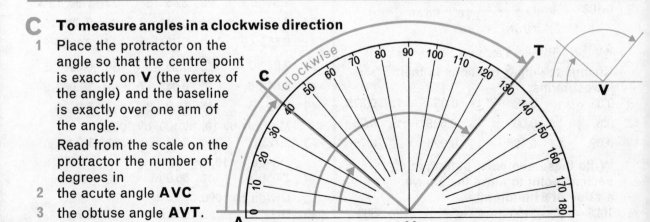

Measuring angles   180° protractor

A Measure these angles in a clockwise direction using your 180° protractor.

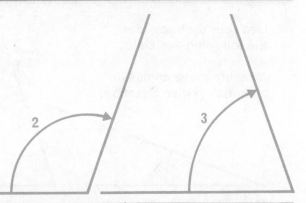

B **To measure angles in an anticlockwise direction**

The protractor is placed on the angles to be measured, as before.

Counting anticlockwise, how many 10° divisions are there in:

1 the acute angle **EVD**

2 the obtuse angle **EVF**?

Write in degrees the size of:

3 the acute angle **EVD**

4 the obtuse angle **EVF**.

It is easier to read the scale on a protractor if it is numbered anticlockwise as well as clockwise.

C Remember When two angles together make 180°, they are called **supplementary angles**.

1 Copy this chart and fill in the supplementary angle in each case.

0°	10°	20°	30°	40°	50°	60°	70°	80°	90°	100°	110°	120°	130°	140°	150°	160°	170°	180°
180°	170°																10°	0°

Notice that each pair of angles in the table adds up to 180°.

2 Give a reason for this..

3 Mark each supplementary angle on your protractor.

There will be two numbers for each division, as shown.

Measure **clockwise**

4 angle **BVA**   5   angle **BVT**.

Measure **anticlockwise**

6 angle **SVT**   7   angle **SVA**.

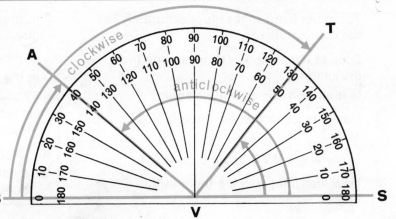

The protractor measuring angles

A Use your protractor for the following exercises.

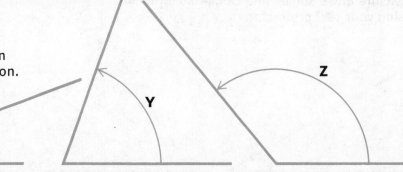

1 Measure these angles in an anticlockwise direction.

2 **Measure clockwise.**
Draw and mark these angles.
20°   50°   80°   120°   150°   170°

3 **Measure anticlockwise.**
Draw and mark these angles.
10°   40°   60°   90°   110°   160°

4 Write the angle which is supplementary to each of the angles in **2** and **3**.

5 Draw a horizontal, a vertical and an oblique straight line and mark each of them **AB**.

6 On each line, with **A** as the vertex, draw in an anticlockwise direction an angle of:
a   50°   b   100°.

7 On each line, with **B** as the vertex, draw in a clockwise direction an angle of:
a   30°   b   150°.

B The protractor shown in the drawing is made of clear plastic.

1 Give a reason why this is so.

The degrees are numbered in tens 0, 10, 20 . . . 180

a   clockwise on the outer edge

b   anticlockwise on the inner edge.

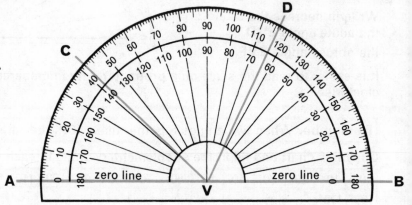

You must learn to measure accurately to the nearest degree.

Look at the angle **AVC** marked on the protractor.

2 Is it an acute or an obtuse angle?

3 How many degrees are there in this angle?

4 Is the angle **BVC** acute or obtuse?

5 How many degrees are there in this angle?

In the same way, read from the scale the number of degrees:

6 in the angle marked **AVD**

7 in the angle marked **BVD**.

Before drawing or measuring an angle, it is important to think whether the angle is:

a   larger or smaller than a right angle

b   measured in a clockwise or an anticlockwise direction.

The protractor measuring, drawing angles

A

1. Get a protractor marked in degrees. For each angle below, think whether the angle is
   a larger or smaller than a right angle   b to be measured clockwise or anticlockwise.

2. Measure each angle as accurately as possible.

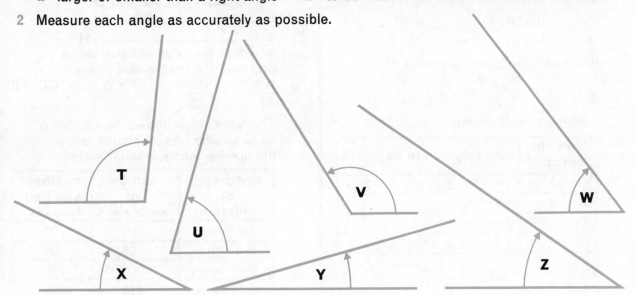

3. Find the angle which is supplementary to each of the angles.

B

Angles may be named by three capital letters, the middle one being placed at the vertex.
The symbol which stands for 'angle' is ∠ or ∧.
For example, the angle **ABC** is written as ∠ **ABC** or **A$\hat{B}$C**.

Measure:
1. ∠ **ABC**   2. **X$\hat{Y}$Z**
3. ∠ **EFG**   4. **A$\hat{O}$B**.

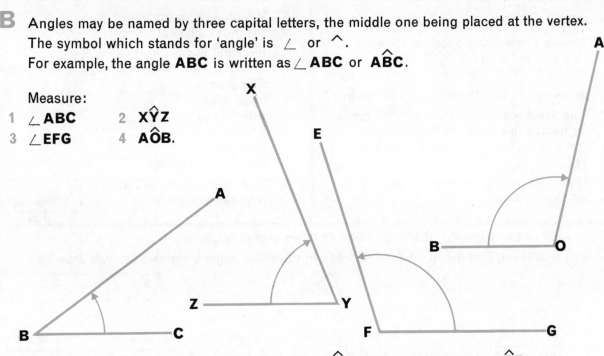

5. Draw and letter these angles. ∠ **HOK**=128° **S$\hat{T}$R**=53° ∠ **VWX**=25° **N$\hat{O}$P**=146°

6. Find the angle which is supplementary to each of these angles.

Making sure

A

Copy and complete:

1 $10^1 = 10 = \square$

2 $10^2 = 10 \times 10 = \square$

3 $10^3 = 10 \times 10 \times 10 = \square$

4 $10^4 = 10 \times 10 \times 10 \times 10 = \square$.

In the same way, find the value of:

5 2^1 2^2 2^3 2^4 2^5 2^6

6 3^1 3^2 3^3 3^4 3^5 3^6.

Find the correct change in each case.

	amount spent	money given in payment
7	37p+49½p	1 FIFTY, 2 TENS, 4 FIVES
8	82p+57p	3 FIFTIES
9	£1·98+61p	3 £1 notes
10	£1·80×3	3 £1 notes, 5 FIFTIES

Through how many degrees does the minute-hand of the clock turn in:

11 1h   12 15 min

13 5 min   14 1 min?

Through how many degrees does the minute-hand turn in:

15 30 min   16 20 min   17 45 min

18 35 min   19 10 min   20 55 min?

Find the number of degrees in the angle formed by the hands of the clock

21 at 4 o'clock   22 at 7 o'clock.

23 There are two answers to each question **21** and **22**. Find both and say why there are two answers.

B

1 Measure each of these lines in mm.

A ———————————————— B

C ———————————— D

E ——————— F

G ———————————— H

Now find the value of these ratios expressed in their lowest terms.

2 $\dfrac{AB}{EF}$ 3 $\dfrac{GH}{AB}$ 4 EF:CD   5 CD:AB

The table below shows the number of children who had swimming lessons and the number who learned to swim.

age group of children	number of swimmers	number who had lessons
7–8 years	120	200
8–9 years	195	300
9–10 years	200	250
10–11 years	210	300

6 Find the percentage of swimmers in each age group.

Which age group was:

7 the most successful

8 the least successful?

The plan is of an area which is to be covered with slabs each 0.5 m square.

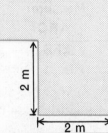

9 How many slabs will be required altogether?

C

In each of the drawings, the size of one or more angles is given.

1 By calculation, find the number of degrees in the other angle or angles in each drawing.

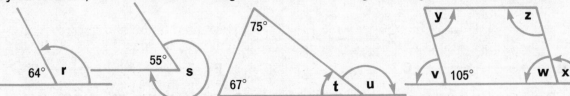

2 Draw a circle of 48 mm radius and construct a hexagon within the circle.

3 Find in mm the length of a line joining two opposite corners of the hexagon.

Making sure

A

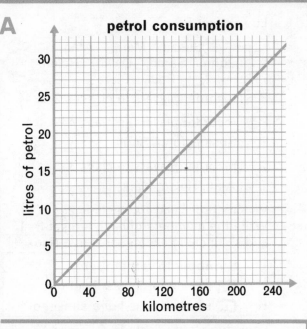

petrol consumption

litres of petrol (vertical axis: 0, 5, 10, 15, 20, 25, 30)

kilometres (horizontal axis: 0, 40, 80, 120, 160, 200, 240)

The graph shows the petrol consumption of a car which uses petrol at the rate of 5 litres per 40 km.

What is represented by one small division on:
1 the horizontal axis   2 the vertical axis?

From the graph, find how far the car will travel on:
3 20 litres   4 14 litres   5 27 litres.

What quantities of petrol will be used on journeys of:
6 200 km   7 88 km   8 232 km?

Check the answers to questions **3** to **8** by calculation.

9 Draw a graph to show petrol consumption at a rate of 10 litres per 100 kilometres.

B

The table gives the heights of five children and the mass of four of them.

name	height	mass
Louise	1.57 m	33.8 kg
James	1.45 m	
John	1.55 m	34.6 kg
Jane	1.47 m	35.2 kg
Anna	1.46 m	33.8 kg

1 Find the average height of the children.
2 The average mass of the five children is 33.9 kg.
What is James's mass?

Each of the diagrams below is half of a symmetrical pattern.

Copy each on squared paper and complete it.

Show by dotted lines all the lines of symmetry.

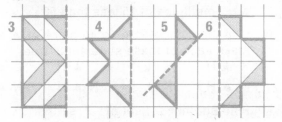

C

1 Find the largest possible whole number that can be written in place of each letter.
$(5 \times q) + 3 < 39$ $(8 \times r) + 6 < 63$
$(9 \times s) - 4 < 55$ $(t \times 7) - 2 < 34$
$(u \times 6) - 2 < 59$ $(v \times 4) - 3 < 35$

2 Name each angle.

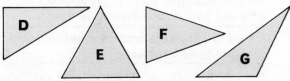

Name each triangle:
3 by its angles   4 by its sides.

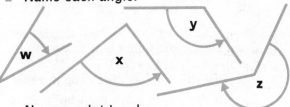

How many h and min from:
5 10.17 a.m. to noon   10 23.16 to 01.54
6 midnight to 6.15 a.m.   11 09.15 to 13.00
7 4.15 p.m. to 7.18 p.m.   12 23.42 to 01.50
8 9.53 p.m. to 11.07 p.m.   13 08.33 to 14.10
9 9.35 a.m. to 3.13 p.m.   14 22.25 to 02.15?

Sets and subsets

The drawing shows the set of British coins.
The set can be enclosed in brackets.
C={British coins}

1 Name the members of set C.

You can make a diagram of this set by enclosing the members in a ring.

C halfpenny, penny, TWO, FIVE, TEN, FIFTY

How many members of set C are:
2 'bronze' coins 3 'silver' coins?

4 Draw and complete the diagrams below, naming the members of each of the sets.
B={British 'bronze' coins}
S={British 'silver' coins}

B S

5 Draw similar diagrams and name the members of these sets.
L={British coins less than 10p in value}
G={British coins more than 5p in value}

Look carefully at the members of the sets B, S, L and G. You find that these sets are part of and belong to set C.

> They are **sets within a set** and are called **subsets**.

Sets B, S, L, G are all subsets of set C.

6 Draw diagrams and name the members of three subsets of set M.
M={measures used in school}

M km, mℓ, mm, ℓ, m, g, cm, kg

Look at set R.

R Susan, Mark, Alan, John, Sarah, David, Helen, Paul, Clare

R={recorder players in classes 2, 3, 4}

P={recorder players in class 4}

P={Susan, John, Sarah}

T={recorder players in class 3}

T={Alan, Helen, Mark}

V={recorder players in class 2}

7 Write the members of each subset P, T and V. Enclose each subset in a ring.

> **Symbols to remember**
> $\subset$ stands for 'is a subset of'
> $\not\subset$ stands for 'is not a subset of'

Look again at the sets R, P, T and V.

8 Show by using the symbol $\subset$ that each of the sets P, T and V is a subset of R. The first one is done for you. P $\subset$ R

Look at the sets below.
Z={2, 4, 6, 8, 10, 12}
A={2, 4} B={10}
C={1, 2, 3} D={10, 12, 14, 16}
E={12, 10, 4} F={8, 9, 10}

9 Use the symbols $\subset$ or $\not\subset$ in place of ▲ to make each of these statements true.
A ▲ Z B ▲ Z C ▲ Z
D ▲ Z E ▲ Z F ▲ Z

Look carefully at these sets.
H={3, 6, 9, . . . 60}
J={5, 10, 15, 20, . . .}
K={multiples of 9 less than 60}
L={multiples of 3 less than 60}
M={multiples of 5 less than 60}
N={multiples of 15 less than 60}

10 Use the symbol $\subset$ or $\not\subset$ in place of ▲ to make each of these statements true.
K ▲ H K ▲ J L ▲ H L ▲ J
M ▲ H M ▲ J N ▲ H N ▲ J

11 Find another subset of: set H set J

Sets and subsets

A

Tor School Library
Opening times 3.30 p.m. – 4 p.m. daily

Librarians
David Hall   Ann Smith   Paul Stanton
Jane Ross   Steven Brown

1 Draw a ring diagram to show the members of
L = {librarians at Tor School}.

How many of the members are:

2 girls   3 boys?

4 Draw a ring diagram to show the members of
B = {boys who are librarians}.

Look at set B and set L. You see that

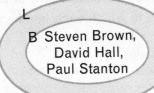

B ⊂ L which is shown by drawing this diagram.

5 Write the names which can be put in the coloured part of the diagram.

F = {girls who are librarians}.

6 Draw a diagram to show that F ⊂ L.

7 Write the names which can be put in the coloured part of this diagram.

B

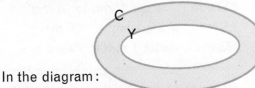

In the diagram:
C = {the boys and girls in class 6}
Y = {the girls under 10 years of age}
Y ⊂ C.

1 What can be shown in the shaded part of the diagram?

In which part of the diagram:
a the shaded   **b** the unshaded part
would these names be written?

2 John aged 9   3 Rachel aged 9
4 Susan aged 11   5 Peter aged 10

C The diagram shows set S and set R.

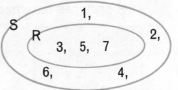

R ⊂ S

Write and complete the following, putting the symbol ∈ or ∉ in place of ▲.

1 2 ▲ S   2 3 ▲ R   3 2 ▲ R
4 3 ▲ S   5 6 ▲ S   6 4 ▲ R
7 6 ▲ R   8 5 ▲ S   9 1 ▲ R

In the diagram:
L = {all the letters of the alphabet}
V = {vowels}.

10 Draw the diagram to show V ⊂ L and write in the members of both sets.

D Draw diagrams to show the following sets and subsets.
In each case, write the members in the diagram.

1 W = {whole numbers between 1 and 13}
E = {even numbers between 1 and 13}
E ⊂ W

2 K = {multiples of 3 less than 40}
H = {multiples of 6 less than 40}
H ⊂ K

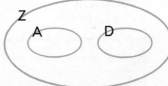

In the diagram:
Z = {whole numbers between 3 and 21}
A = {prime numbers between 3 and 21}
D = {square numbers between 3 and 21}
A ⊂ Z   D ⊂ Z.

3 Copy the diagram and show in it the members of Z, A and D.

4 Are any members of subsets A and D common to both of these subsets?

Plans drawing to scale

A These shapes have been drawn to scale.

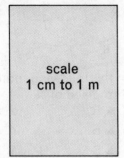

scale
1 cm to 1 m

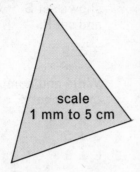

scale
1 mm to 5 cm

1 Measure in cm the length and width of the rectangle.

2 Use the scale to find its actual dimensions.

3 Measure the sides of the triangle in mm.

Find their actual dimensions:

4 in cm   5 in m.

> Scales are also written as **fractions** or as **ratios**, in which case it is important that the **units of measurement are of the same kind.**

For example:

1 cm to 1 m = 1 cm to 100 cm

  = $\frac{1}{100}$ or 1:100

1 mm to 5 cm = 1 mm to 50 mm

  = $\frac{1}{50}$ or 1:50

Write first as a fraction, then as a ratio:

6 1 cm to 2 m   7 1 cm to 8 m

8 1 mm to 50 cm   9 1 mm to 1 m.

B Look at the scale to which each of these lines has been drawn.

1 Measure them and find the length each represents.

m ——————————— scale 1 cm to 20 cm

n ——————— scale 1 mm to 100 mm

o ——————— scale 1 cm to 5 m

p ——————— scale 1 mm to 1 cm

r ——————— scale 1 cm to 10 m

2 Write each of the given scales:
   a as a fraction   b as a ratio.

3 Measure each of the lines below in cm.

4 Find the scale to which each line has been drawn.

5 Write each scale:
   a as a fraction   b as a ratio.

s |←——————————→|
        7 m

t |←——————————→|
       300 m

u |←——————————→|
        55 m

v |←————————→|
       450 m

Using the given scales, draw lines to represent:

6 800 mm   scale 1 mm to 10 mm

7 7.5 m   scale 1 mm to 100 mm

8 163 m   scale 1 mm to 1000 mm.

C

changing room | platform

Plan of hall and changing room

scale
1 mm to 0.5 m   1:500

Using the scale on the plan, find the actual length represented in m by:

1 8 mm   2 20 mm   3 33 mm.

Find the actual length and width in m of:

4 the hall   5 the changing room

6 the platform.

7 What is the area in m² of the platform?

8 Use a set square and a ruler to draw the plan again to the scale 1 mm to 0.25 m   1:250.

Plans   drawing to scale

A Look at this rough sketch of a wood block.

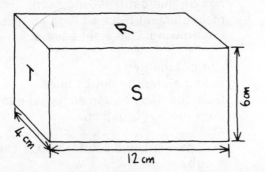

Three faces have been marked **R**, **S** and **T**.

How many faces are the same size:
1 as **R**   2 as **S**   3 as **T**?

4 How many faces are there altogether?

5 What is the shape of each face?

6 Using a ruler and a set square, make a full-size drawing of each of the faces **R**, **S** and **T**.

7 Show the dimensions on each drawing.

B Before making an accurate drawing of an object full size or to scale, you should always make a rough sketch which gives a good idea of its shape and its measurements.

The rough sketch shows the shape and measurements of a biscuit box.

Below the sketch are three accurate scale drawings which show a view of the box seen from:

above   **the front**   **the end** or **side**.

Remember

The view seen from above is the **plan**.

The view seen from the front is the **front elevation**.

The view seen from the end (or side) is the **end elevation**.

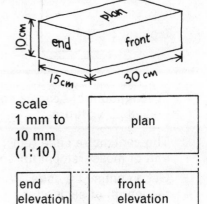

scale
1 mm to
10 mm
(1:10)

Notice that the three accurate scale drawings are arranged in a special order.
1 Copy the plan and the elevations of the biscuit box, but make the scale 1 mm to 5 mm (1:5).

2 From the rough sketch, draw a plan and the front and end elevations to the scale of 1 cm to 10 cm (1:10).

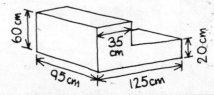

C

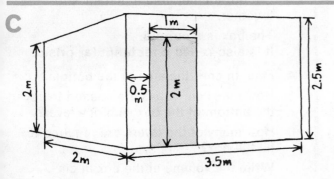

The rough sketch shows the dimensions of a garden shed.

Draw to a scale of 1 mm to 50 mm (1:50)
1 the plan of the shed
2 the front elevation (omit the door)
3 the end elevation.

4 Now draw the front elevation again. This time, use the scale 1 mm to 25 mm (1:25) and show the door.

Solids nets

A

Remember
Solids have three dimensions
length, **breadth**, **thickness** (or **height**).

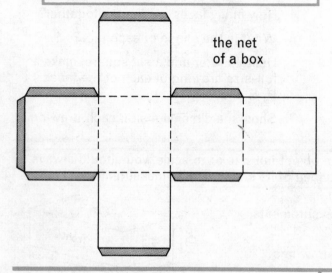

the net
of a box

1 Measure and then draw the net of the box on thin card, making each measurement twice as long as those in the drawing. Use a set square.

2 Cut out the net.
Fold it along the dotted lines.
Gum the flaps or use sticky tape to stick the box together.

You have made a solid which is called a **cube**.

3 What is: a the length   b the breadth   c the height of the cube?

4 What is: a the shape   b the area of each face?

5 How many: a faces   b vertices   c edges has a cube?

B

The amount of space a solid takes up is called its **volume**.

The centimetre cube (cm³) is used as the unit of measurement for some solids.

Get a centimetre cube. What is:
1 the length of each edge
2 the area of each of the six faces?

The drawings show two **square prisms**.

 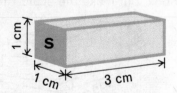

1 cm

S

1 cm   3 cm

In what way is each of the square prisms:
3 similar to a cube
4 different from a cube?
5 How many centimetre cubes would be fitted together to make the square prism marked **S**? What is its volume in cm³?
6 Make a sketch of a square prism made up of 14 centimetre cubes.
7 Write: a its length, breadth and height
       b its volume in cm³.

C

The drawing is the net of a rectangular box with an open top.

1 Write its length, breadth and height.

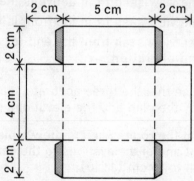

2 cm   5 cm   2 cm

2 cm

4 cm

2 cm

2 On thin card, draw the net and the flaps.

3 Cut out the net, fold it and stick it together.

The box is a **cuboid**.
It is also called a **rectangular prism**.

4 Find, in cm², the area of the bottom.
5 How many cm cubes are needed to cover the bottom of the box with one layer?
6 How many of the layers are required to fill the box?
7 Write the volume of the box in cm³.

Solids volume

A These cuboids are made up of centimetre cubes.

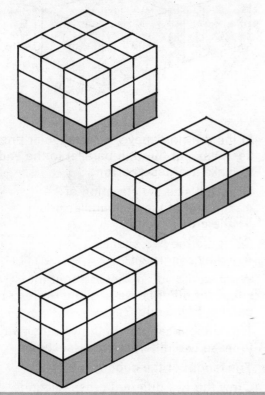

1 What is the length, the breadth and the height of the large cube?

2 How many centimetre cubes are there in each layer of the large cube?

3 How many layers are there?

4 What is the volume of the large cube in cm³?

5 Look at the square prism. Write its length, breadth and height.

6 How many cm³ are there in each layer?

7 How many layers are there?

8 What is the volume in cm³ of the square prism?

9 Find:
  a the dimensions of the rectangular prism
  b its volume in cm³.

10 Get 8 centimetre cubes and use them to make:
  a a cube   b a square prism
  c a rectangular prism.

11 Sketch each solid and show its dimensions.

12 What is the volume of each of the solids?

13 Using 18 centimetre cubes, make as many cuboids as you can.

14 Write the dimensions of each of these cuboids.

B

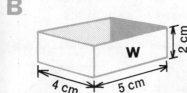
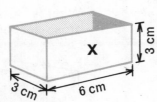
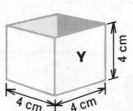
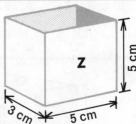

The inside measurements of boxes **W**, **X**, **Y** and **Z** are shown.

1 What is the name of the shape of each of these boxes?

2 How many cm³ can be fitted into the bottom layer of box **W**?

3 How many layers are needed to fill the box?

4 Write: The volume of box **W** is ☐ cm³.

5 In the same way, find the volume of each of the boxes **X**, **Y** and **Z**.

Which of the boxes has:
6 the largest volume
7 the smallest volume?

8 Write the shortest method by which you can find the volume of a solid when you know:
its length, breadth and height in cm.

Find the volume of each of these cuboids.

	9	10	11	12	13
length	8 cm	9 cm	10 cm	3 cm	6 cm
breadth	7 cm	4 cm	3 cm	2.5 cm	3.4 cm
height	3 cm	6 cm	7 cm	4 cm	5 cm

Solids cross-sections

A

The drawing shows a wooden cube.

What do you know about:

1 its edges
2 its angles?
3 Name the shape of each face.
4 Are these shapes congruent?
5 Draw full size the end elevation of the cube.

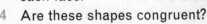

This drawing shows the cube cut through parallel to the end to make a **cross-section**.

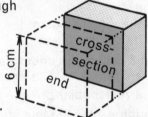

6 Draw full size the end elevation of this cross-section.
7 Now compare it with the drawing for **A5**. What do you discover?
8 If other cross-sections were cut parallel to the end, would the shape of each be congruent?
9 Show, by a drawing, another way the cube can be cut to make a cross-section.
10 What is the shape of this cross-section?

B

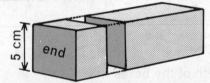

In this drawing, a square prism has been cut through, parallel to the end to make a **cross-section**.

Draw full size the elevation of:
1 the end   2 the cross-section.
3 Are the two shapes congruent?
4 Would the shapes of other cross-sections cut parallel to the end be congruent?
5 The square prism can be cut in other ways to make a cross-section. Show one way by a drawing.
6 What is the shape of this cross-section?

C

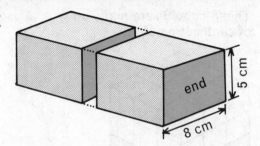

In the drawing above, a rectangular prism has been cut through parallel to the end to make a **cross-section**.

1 Draw full size the elevation of:
a the end of the rectangular prism
b the cross-section.
2 Compare the two shapes. Are they congruent?
3 What would you discover about the shapes if other cross-sections were cut parallel to the ends?

This cuboid can be cut in two other ways to make two different cross-sections.

The length of the cuboid is 9 cm.

4 Draw the two different cross-sections and mark the lengths of the sides.
5 What is the shape of each of the cross-sections?

D

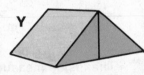

The two prisms shown in the drawings were each made from a 10 cm cube.

Describe how:
1 the prism marked **X** was made
2 the prism marked **Y** was made.

Find:
3 the length, breadth and height of prism **X**;
4 the length, breadth and height of prism **Y**.
5 What is the volume of each prism?
6 Name each of the prisms.

Solids nets, cross-sections

A The drawing is the net of a prism, the two ends of which are equilateral triangles of 6 cm sides.

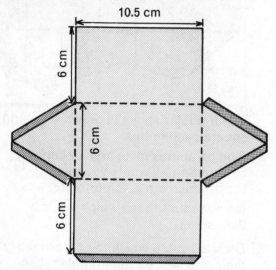

10.5 cm

6 cm

6 cm

6 cm

1 On thin card, draw the net to the given size. Do not forget the flaps.

2 Cut out the net.
Fold it along the dotted lines and gum the flaps to stick the prism together.

The solid you have made is called a **triangular prism**.

Write and complete:

3 The triangular prism has ☐ faces, ☐ vertices and ☐ edges.

What is the shape of:

4 the bottom   5 the two sides?

6 Use compasses and a ruler to draw full size the end elevation of the prism.

In the drawing below, a triangular prism has been cut to show a cross-section.

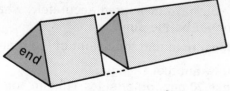

7 What is the shape of the cross-section?

8 Are the shapes of the end elevation and the cross-section congruent?

B From the drawing of the open-ended cylinder, find:

1 the shape of the two ends

2 its diameter and length.

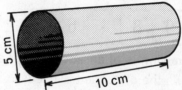

5 cm

10 cm

3 Using π=3.14, find the circumference of the cylinder.

4 Draw full size, the net of the cylinder and mark a flap.

5 Cut out the net. Gum the flap and stick the cylinder together.

The wooden cylinder below has been cut to show a cross-section.

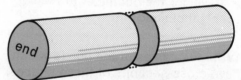

end

6 What is the shape of the cross-section?

7 Are the shapes of the end elevation and the cross-section congruent?

> **Remember** A cross-section is cut parallel to one of the faces of the solid.

C The drawings below are the plans and end elevations of five solids about which you have learned.

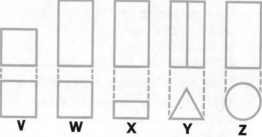

V   W   X   Y   Z

1 Write the name of each of the solids.

2 Give some examples of objects which are similar in shape to these solids.

3 Make a sketch of each of the solids.

Making sure

A Turn to pages 7 and 8.
Work sections **A** to **E** as quickly as
possible. Mark the answers and correct
any mistakes.

B

1	9	8	4	6	7

The drawing is of an odometer of a car.

It shows the distance travelled
in km and tenths of a km.

Write the distance travelled:

1 in figures   2 in words.

3 How many metres must be travelled to
change the **6** into **7**?

4 How many km must be travelled before
the **4** changes to **5**?

5 How many more km has the car
to travel for the odometer to read
twenty thousand km?

C Write the names of the solids which
have cross-sections of these shapes.

Peter built three square prisms, each
from 36 centimetre cubes.

5 What were the dimensions, the length
breadth and height, of each?

6 Measure in mm
the diameter of
this circle.

7 Find the length of
its circumference
to the nearest cm.
($\pi = 3.14$)

8 Draw a circle with a radius of 35 mm.

9 With the same centre, draw two more
circles, increasing the radius by 8 mm
for each.

10 Find the diameter of the largest circle.

> Circles with the same centre are called
> **concentric circles**.

D

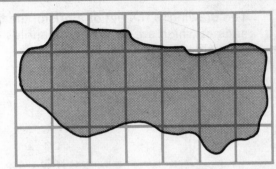

The irregular shape is drawn on a grid of
square centimetres.

1 Find its approximate area in cm²
by counting as whole squares
those which are a half or more.

Do not count those which are less
than a half.

2 Draw a square which is approximately
the same area as the irregular shape.

3 What is the area of a square of 5 cm side?

E

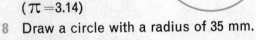

1 Draw a triangle to the given dimensions.
Letter the vertices as shown.

2 Use a protractor to measure as accurately
as possible the size of each angle.
Write: $A\hat{B}C = \square°$ $\angle BAC = \square°$ $A\hat{C}B = \square°$.

3 Find the sum of the three angles.

4 If you have measured accurately, what
should be the sum?

5 Measure in mm the height of the triangle.

6 Draw another triangle:
base 70 mm, other sides 115 mm and
63 mm. Letter it XYZ.

7 Measure: $X\hat{Y}Z$ $X\hat{Z}Y$ $Y\hat{X}Z$.

8 Measure the height of the triangle.

Making sure

A Turn to pages 13 and 14.
Work sections **A** to **E** as quickly as possible. Mark the answers and correct any mistakes.

B Write these numbers in figures.
1 thirty thousand and eighty-four
2 807 tenths   3 509 hundredths
4 thirteen thousand and six
5 two hundred thousand and seventy
6 $(6 \times 10^4) + (0 \times 10^3) + (2 \times 10^2) + (7 \times 10^1)$

Find the missing numbers in the table. The first has been done for you.

7	$\frac{9}{20}$	$\frac{45}{100}$	0.45	45%
8	$\frac{16}{25}$	$\frac{\square}{100}$	$\square$	$\square$%
9	$\frac{\square}{50}$	$\frac{54}{100}$	$\square$	$\square$%
10	$\frac{11}{\square}$	$\frac{\square}{100}$	0.55	$\square$%
11	$\frac{\square}{50}$	$\frac{\square}{100}$	$\square$	62%
12	$\frac{17}{20}$	$\frac{\square}{100}$	$\square$	$\square$%
13	$\frac{7}{\square}$	$\frac{28}{100}$	$\square$	$\square$%
14	$\frac{\square}{20}$	$\frac{\square}{100}$	0.35	$\square$%
15	$\frac{11}{\square}$	$\frac{\square}{100}$	$\square$	44%

C Find the value of:
1 50% of 350   5 20% of 845
2 25% of 656   6 10% of 85p
3 10% of £2·30   7 15% of 1 kg
4 5% of £2·30   8 35% of 1 ℓ.

Increase by 10%:
9 950   10 45p   11 £4·60.

Decrease by 25%:
12 792   13 94p   14 £70·20.

A record-player costs £70. It can be paid for by a 10% deposit and the remainder in 10 equal instalments. Find:
15 the deposit   16 one instalment.

By rounding off the numbers, find the approximate answers to:
17 79×29 18 9.8×47 19 $4\frac{7}{8} \times 16$
20 $£3·90 \times 22$ 21 0.45×71 22 57×45.
23 Find the correct answer in each case.

D Look at the rectangle **X**.

Find:
1 the perimeter in cm
2 the area in cm².

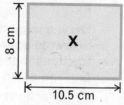

3 Find the length of a rectangle of the same area as rectangle **X**, but with a width of 7 cm.
4 What is the sum of the angles of a quadrilateral?
5 Three of the angles of a quadrilateral are 100°, 110° and 90°. Find the fourth angle.

Find each missing measurement.

	mm	m
6	3037	
7		2.9
8	850	
9		6.035

	g	kg
14		3.73
15	800	
16		0.6
17	4420	

	m	km
10		1.6
11	7405	
12		10.5
13	935	

	mℓ	ℓ
18	350	
19		5.25
20	8070	
21		9.125

E Find the cost of each of these shopping items.
1 2 kg 500 g at 18p per $\frac{1}{2}$ kg
2 1 kg 800 g at 60p per kg
3 5.5 kg at 9p per 100 g
4 750 g at £3·20 per kg
5 4.25 kg at 80p per kg

Multiply: a by 10   b by 100
6 740   7 27.5   8 30.09   9 1.708.

Multiply by 1000:
10 0.4   11 28   12 1.23   13 0.041.

Divide: a by 10   b by 100
14 1.6   15 3120   16 29.2   17 4.0.

Divide by 1000:
18 17   19 486   20 9933   21 10.

Making sure

A

$F = \{\frac{1}{3}, \frac{2}{5}, \frac{7}{8}, \frac{3}{10}, \frac{1}{6}, \frac{3}{8}, \frac{9}{10}, \frac{1}{10}\}$

1 Draw a large diagram, like the one below, to show set F and write the fractions in the correct subsets.
G = {fractions greater than $\frac{3}{4}$}
L = {fractions less than $\frac{1}{4}$}

2 Which of the fractions should be written in the shaded part?

3 Use the symbol ⊂ to show the subsets of F.

W = {1, 2, 3, . . . 24, 25, 26}

4 Draw a large diagram to show set W and the following subsets of W.
S = {square numbers less than 26}
P = {prime numbers less than 26}
T = {multiples of 10 less than 26}
Enter the numbers in the diagram.

B

The inside measurements of the box are given in the diagram.

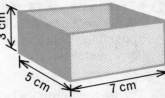

1 How many centimetre cubes can be fitted into the bottom of the box?

2 Find the volume of the box in cm³.

The inside measurements of a tank are 30 cm long, 20 cm wide and 10 cm deep.

3 Find the volume of the tank in cm³.

4 Water is put into the tank to within 2 cm of the top.
Find in cm³ the volume of the water.

5 What is the mass of the water in kg? (1000 cm³ of water has a mass of 1 kg.)

Find the volume of each of these cuboids

	6	7	8	9	10
length	11 cm	9 cm	4.5 cm	10 cm	7 cm
breadth	6 cm	5 cm	3 cm	10 cm	4 cm
height	6 cm	12 cm	4 cm	20 cm	2.5 cm

C

Bearings are measured from North in a clockwise direction.

Use a protractor to find the bearing from Kempton to:

1 Ampton   2 Compton   3 Lipton.

The distances from Kempton 'as the crow flies' are: to Ampton 45 km, to Compton 30 km, to Lipton 28 km.

4 Draw, to a scale of 1 cm to 5 km, a map showing the positions of the four places.

Using your map, find, by measuring, the approximate distance in km 'as the crow flies' from:

5 Ampton to Compton

6 Compton to Lipton

7 Lipton to Ampton.

1 cm to 1 m as a ratio is 1:100.

Now write and complete:

8 1 cm to 1 km as a ratio is □:□

9 1 cm to 5 km as a ratio is □:□.